John Lennon In His Own Words.

Compiled by Miles.
Designed by
Pearce Marchbank.

quick fox

New York / London

Exclusive distributors:
Quick Fox,
33 West 60th Street
New York, N.Y. 10023, USA.
Book Sales Limited, 78 Newman Street,
London W1P 3LA
Book Sales Pty. Limited,
27 Clarendon Street, Artarmon, Sydney,
NSW 2064, Australia.
Music Sales Gmbh,
Kölner Strasse 199, D-5000,
Cologne 90, West Germany

Series editor and art director:
Pearce Marchbank

ISBN: 0-8256-3953-0
030953

Printed in the United States of America.

1945.

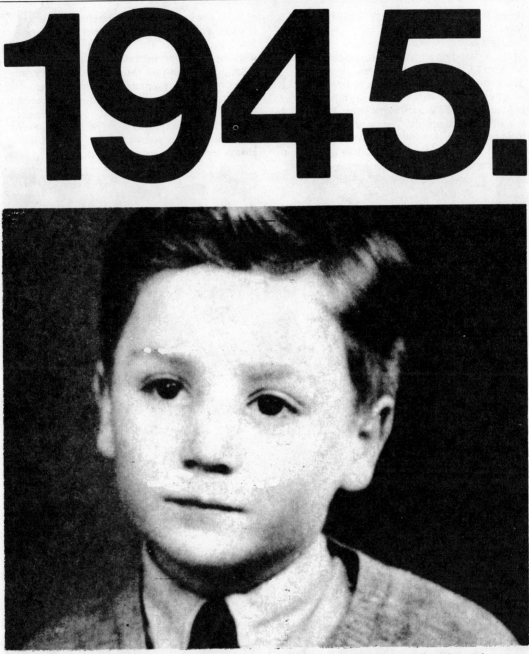

John went to Dovedale Primary School: I fought my way through Dovedale. I learned lots of dirty jokes very young. There was this girl who told me them. The gang I led went in for shoplifting and pulling girls' knickers down. Other boys' parents hated me. Most of the masters hated me.

I soon forgot my father. But I did see my mother now and again. I often thought about her, though I never realized for a long time that she was living no more than five or ten miles away.

Childhood: Strawberry Fields is a real place. After I stopped living at Penny Lane, I moved in with my auntie who lived in the suburbs in a nice semidetached place with a small garden and doctors and lawyers and that ilk living around — not the poor slummy kind of image that was projected in all the Beatles stories. In the class system, it was about half a class higher than Paul, George and Ringo, who lived in governmment-subsidized housing. We owned our house and had a garden. They didn't have anything like that. Near that home was Strawberry Fields, a house near a boys' reformatory where I used to go to garden parties as a kid with my friends Nigel and Pete. We would go there and hang out and sell lemonade bottles for a penny. We always had fun at Strawberry Fields. So that's where I got the name. But I used it as an image. Strawberry Fields forever.

Living is easy — With eyes closed. Misunderstanding all you see. It still goes, doesn't it? Aren't I saying exactly the same thing now? The awareness apparently trying to be expressed is — let's say in one way I was always hip. I was hip in kindergarten. I was different from the others. I was different all my life. The second verse goes, "No one I think is in my tree." Well, I was too shy and self-doubting. Nobody seems to be as hip as me is what I was saying. Therefore, I must be crazy or a genius — "I mean it must be high or low," the next line. There was something wrong with me, I thought, because I seemed to see things other people didn't see. I thought I was crazy or an egomaniac for claiming to see things other people didn't see. As a child, I would say, *But this is going on!* and everybody would look at me as if I was crazy. I always was so psychic or intuitive or poetic or whatever you want to call it, that I was always seeing things in a hallucinatory way.

JOHN WITH HIS MOTHER, JULIA.

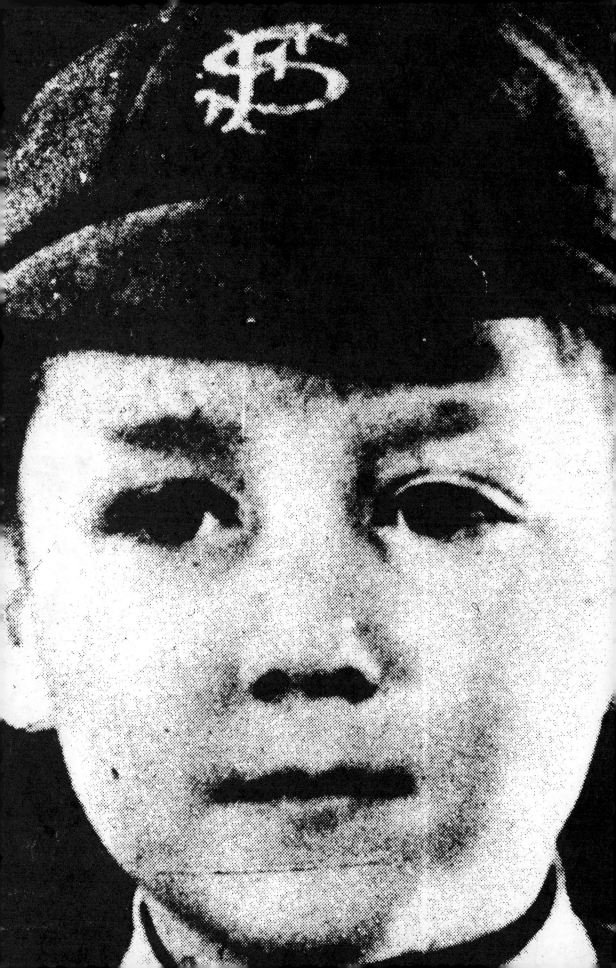

1952.

1952: John went to Quarrybank Grammar School:
I looked at the hundreds of new kids and thought,
Christ, I'll have to fight my way through all this
lot. The first fight I got in I lost. I lost me nerve
when I got really hurt.

At Quarrybank Grammer: I'd been honest at
Dovedale, if nothing else. But I began to realize
that was foolish. So I started lying about
everything.

People like me are aware of their so-called
genius at ten, eight, nine. I always wondered,
"why has nobody discovered me?" In school,
didn't they see that I'm cleverer than anybody in
this school? That the teachers are stupid, too?
That all they had was information that I didn't
need.

I got fuckin' lost in being at Grammar school. I
used to say to me auntie "You throw my fuckin'
poetry out, and you'll regret it when I'm
famous," and she threw the bastard stuff out.

I never forgave her for not treating me like a
fuckin' genius or whatever I was, when I was a
child. It was obvious to me. Why didn't they put
me in art school? Why didn't they train me? Why
would they keep forcing me to be a fuckin'
cowboy like the rest of them? I was different, I
was always different. Why didn't anybody notice
me?

A couple of teachers would notice me,
encourage me to be something or other, to draw
or to paint — express myself. But most of the time
they were trying to beat me into being a fuckin'
dentist or a teacher. And then the fuckin' fans
tried to beat me into being a fuckin' Beatle or an
Engelbert Humperdinck, and the critics tried to
beat me into being Paul McCartney.

Genius: When I was about twelve I used to think I
must be a genius, but nobody's noticed. If there is
such a thing as genius I am one, and if there isn't I
don't care.

Childhood Visions: It was scary as a child, because
there was nobody to relate to. Neither my auntie
nor my friends nor anybody could ever see what I
did. It was very, very scary and the only contact I
had was reading about an Oscar Wilde or a Dylan
Thomas or a van Gogh — all those books
that my auntie had that talked about their
suffering because of their visions. Because of what
they saw, they were tortured by society for trying
to express what they were. I *saw* loneliness.

Surrealism had a great effect on me, because
then I realized that my imagery and my mind
wasn't insanity; that if it was insane, I belong in
an exclusive club that sees the world in those
terms. Surrealism to me is reality. Psychic vision
to me is reality. Even as a child. When I looked at
myself in the mirror or when I was 12, 13, I used
to literally trance out into alpha. I didn't know
what it was called then. I found out years later
there's a name for those conditions. But I would
find myself seeing hallucinatory images of my face
changing and becoming cosmic and complete. It
caused me to always be a rebel. This thing gave me
a chip on the shoulder; but, on the other hand, I
wanted to be loved and accepted. Part of me
would like to be accepted by all facets of society
and not be this loudmouthed lunatic musician.
But I cannot be what I am not.

**John learned to play the harmonica as his first
instrument:** I can't remember why I took it up in
the first place — I must have picked one up very
cheap. I know we used to take in students and one
of them had a mouth organ and said he'd buy me
one if I could learn a tune by the next morning. So
I learned about two. I was somewhere between
eight and twelve at the time — in shorts pants
anyway. Another time I was travelling to
Edinburgh on me own to see me auntie and I
played the mouth organ all the way up on the bus.
The driver liked it and told me to meet him at a
place in Edinburgh the next morning and he'd give
me a good mouth organ.

John's schoolteachers: They were all stupid
teachers, except one or two. I always felt I'd make
it. I had to be a millionaire. If I couldn't do it
without being crooked, then I'd have to be
crooked. But I was too much of a coward to be a
crook. I did plan to knock off a shop with another
bloke, do it properly for a change. We used to
look at shops at night, but we never got around to
doing it.

1955.

1955: The Quarrymen: We eventually formed our -selves into a group from school. Our first appearance was in Rose Street — it was their Empire Day celebration. We didn't get paid. We played at blokes' parties after that, or weddings, perhaps got a few bob. But mostly we just played for fun.

John's mother taught him the banjo: I started with a banjo when I was fifteen, when my mother taught me some banjo chords. I played the guitar when I was young like a banjo, with the sixth string hanging loose! I always thought Lonnie and Elvis were great, and all I ever wanted to do was to vamp. I got some banjo things off okay, then

George and Paul came along and taught me other things. My first guitar cost me ten pounds — it was one of those advertised in a paper you send away for. Why did I get it? Oh — the usual kid's disire to get up on stage, I suppose. And also my mother said she could play any stringed instrument. She did teach me a bit...most of our stuff in the early days was twelve-bar stuff. I'd play boogie and George would play lead. I'd vamp like Bruce Welch does, in that style of rhythm.

Rock and Roll Roots: I used to borrow a guitar at first. I couldn't play, but a pal of mine had one and it fascinated me. Eventually my mother bought me one from one of these mail order firms. I suppose it was a bit crummy, when you think about it. But I played it all the time and I got a lot of pracitce. After a while we formed The Quarrymen with a lad named Eric Griffiths, PeteShotton — my best mate at school — and myself. We also had a lad named Gary, who's now an architect, and somebody else named Ivan (Vaughan). Ivan went to the same school as Paul and he brought him along one day when we were playing at a garden fete....shortly after that we started to do big beat numbers like ''Twenty Flight Rock'' — funny, really, because we were meant to be a skiffle group. ''Let's Have A Party'' used to be my big number. I used to sing Lonnie Donegan songs to keep my hand in, though I found I was getting to like Chuck Berry's material more than anything else. It was Elvis who really got me buying records. I thought that early stuff of his was great. The Bill Haley era passed me by, in a way. When his records came on the wireless, my mother used to hear them, but they didn't do anything for me. It was Elvis who got me hooked for beat music. When I heard ''Heartbreak Hotel'', I thought ''this is it'' and I started to grow side-boards and all that gear....I was just drifting. I wouldn't study at school.

June 15, 1955: Enter Paul McCartney: There was a friend of mine called Ivan who lived at the back of my house and he went to the same school as Paul McCartney — The Liverpool Institute High School. It was through Ivan that I first met Paul. Seems that he knew Paul was always dickering around in music and thought that he would be a good lad to have in the group.

So one day when we were playing at Woolton he brought him along. We can both remember it quite well. We've even got the date down. It was June 15th 1955. The Quarrymen were playing on a raised platform and there was a good crowd because it was a warm sunny day.

I'd been kingpin up to then. Now, I thought, if I take him on, what will happen? But he was good. He also looked like Elvis.

I had a group, I was the singer and the leader; I met Paul and I made a decision whether to — and he made a decision too — have him in the group: was it better to have a guy who was better than the people I had in, obviously, or not? To make the group stronger or to let me be stronger? That decision was to let Paul in and make the group stronger.

Paul had bought a trumpet and had this wild theory that he'd actually learned how to play the oldie "When The Saints Go Marching In." He just blew away as hard as he could drowning out everything we were trying to do. He thought he was doing a great job on the tune, but we didn't recognise any of it!

We were also starting to get going on the vocal side and that upset Paul. He found that he couldn't play trumpet and sing at the same time. So, the time came when he had to make a big decision. Lucky for us he made the right one and bought a guitar, which he immediately started to play upside down, being left-handed, anyway, he got it sorted out in the end.

Upside-down chords: Paul was always more advanced than I was. He was always a couple of chords ahead and his songs usually had more chords in them. His dad played the piano. He was always playing pop and jazz standards and Paul picked things up from him....after I'd persuaded me mother to send away for a ten pound guaranteed-not-to-split guitar, she taught me how to play banjo chords on it. That's why in very early photos of the group I'm playing funny chords...Paul told me the chords I had been playing weren't real chords — and his dad said they weren't even banjo chords — though I think they were. Paul had a good guitar at the time. It cost about fourteen pounds. He'd got it in exchange for a trumpet his dad had given him.

When we first started playing together, I learned some chords from Paul and of course he taught me left-handed shapes, so I was playing a sort of upside down version of the correct thing if you can work that one out!

John the drifter: I know I went a bit off the rails when I was about 14. I more or less drifted about, and when I was put in for nine GCE's at school I was a terrible failure.

I was like that all the time I was at school. Art was the only thing I was interested in, and in the end my headmaster said that if I didn't go to art school I might as well become a labourer!

School friends: I think sometimes of the friends who left school at the same time as me, when I made up my mind to go to art school. Some of them went straight to 9 to 5 jobs and within three months they looked like old men. Fat chance of that ever happening to me. The great thing is never to have to be in an office — or anywhere. I like to live on the spur of the moment, I hate to make forward plans.

1957.

October 1957: John entered Art School: I should have been an illustrator, but I found myself in lettering. They might as well have put me in sky-diving. I failed all the exams I stayed on because it was better than working.

I was so concerned with music that I hardly spent any time there. I suppose I was a bit of a contrast to Paul — he liked art too, but he studied his other subjects and got through his exams.

My whole school life was a case of "I couldn't care less". It was just a joke as far as I was concerned. Art was the only thing I could do, and my headmaster told me that if I didn't go to art school I might as well give up life. I wasn't really keen. I thought it would be a crowd of old men, but I should make the effort to try and make something of myself. I stayed for five years doing commercial art. Frankly, I found it all as bad as maths and science. And I loathed those. The funny thing was I didn't even pass art in the GCE. I spent the exam time doing daft cartoons. I got

into art school by doing some decent stuff and taking it along to show them.

During my whole time at art school I just used to disappear from time to time. When my first exam came up, I was with The Beatles in Scotland backing Johnny Gentle. For the second, I was away with the group in Hamburg. Eventually I decided to leave whether I ever passed an exam or not, but when I got back there was a note saying "Don't bother to come back". Believe it or not, I actually got annoyed....don't think I'm proud of it at all. I wouldn't want anybody to follow my example....I was too interested in the easy life, that was my trouble.

Rock and Roll Folk Music: As kids we were all opposed to folk-songs because they were so middle-class. It was all the college students with big scarves and a pint of beer in their hands singing folk songs in what we call la-di-da voices — "I worked in a mine in New-cast-le" and all that shit. There were very few real folk singers you know, though I liked Dominic Behan a bit and

THE QUARRYMEN, WITH PAUL McCARTNEY.

there was some good stuff to be heard in Liverpool. Just occasionally you hear very old records on the radio or TV of real workers in Ireland or somewhere singing these songs and the power of them is fantastic. But mostly folk music is people with fruity voices trying to keep alive somthing thats old and dead. It's all a bit boring like ballet, a minority thing kept going by a minority group. Today's folk song is Rock and Roll. Although it happened to emanate from America, that's not really important in the end because we wrote our own music and that changed everything...

The band played on: There was no point in rehearsing for non-existent dates. But we went on playing together just for kicks. Usually in each other's homes. We kept the record-player going a lot of the time playing the latest American hits. We'd try and get the same effects.

1958.

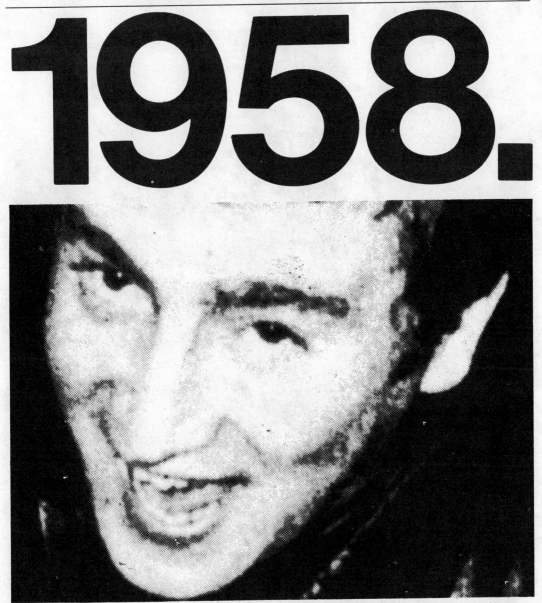

July 15, 1958 John's mother, Julia, was knocked down and killed while waiting at a bus stop: She got killed after visiting my auntie's house where I lived by an off-duty cop who was drunk. I wasn't there at the time. She was just at a bus stop.

The copper came to the door to tell us about the accident. It was just like it's supposed to be, the way it is in the films. Asking if I was her son an all that. Then he told us, and we both went white. It was the worse thing that ever happened to me. I thought, I've no responsibilities to anyone now.

I was sixteen. That was another big trauma for me. I lost her twice. When I was five and I moved in with my auntie, and then when she physically died. That made me more bitter; the chip I had on my shoulder I had as a youth got really big then. I was just re-establishing the relationship with her and she was killed.

After his mother's death: I was in a sort of blind rage for two years. I was either drunk or fighting. It had been the same with other girl friends I'd had. There was something the matter with me.

Because of my attitude, all the other boy's parents, including Paul's father, would say, "Keep away from him." The parents instinctively recognized what I was, which was a troublemaker, meaning I did not conform and I would influence their kids, which I did. I did my best to disrupt every friend's home I had. Partly, maybe, it was out of envy that I didn't have this so-called home. But I really did. I had an auntie and an uncle and a nice suburban home, thank you very much.

There were five women who were my family. Five strong, intelligent women. Five sisters. One happened to be my mother. My mother was the

youngest. She just couldn't deal with life. She had a husband who ran away to sea and the war was on and she couldn't cope with me, and when I was four and a half, I ended up living with her elder sister. Now, those women were fantastic. One day I might do a kind of *Forsyte Saga* just about them. That was my first feminist education.

Anyway, that knowledge and the fact that I wasn't with my parents made me see that parents are not gods. I would infiltrate the other boy's minds. Paul's parents were terrified of me and my influence, simply because I was free from the parents' strangle hold. That was the gift I got for not having parents. I cried a lot about not having them and it was torture, but it also gave me an awareness early. I wasn't an orphan, though. My mother was alive and lived a 15-minute walk away from me all my life. I saw her off and on. I just didn't live with her.

August 29, 1958: George joined The Quarrymen:
Well, from that, Paul introduced me to George, and Paul and I had to make the decision, or I had to make the decision, whether to let George in. I listened to George play, and I said "play 'Raunchy'" or whatever the old story is, and I let him in. I said "O.K, you come in"; that was the three of us then. Then the rest of the group was thrown out gradually. It just happened like that, instead of going for the individual thing, we went for the strongest format, and for equals.

George is ten years younger than me, or some shit like that. I couldn't be bothered with him when he first came around. He used to follow me around like a bloody kid, hanging around all the time, I couldn't be bothered. He was a kid who played guitar, and he was a friend of Paul's which made it all easier. It took me years to come around to him, to start considering him as an equal or anything.

We had all sorts of different drummers all the time, because people who owned drum kits were few and far between; it was an expensive item. Then we got Pet Best, because we needed a drummer to go to Hamburg the next day. We passed the audition on our own with a stray drummer. There are other myths about Pete Best was the Beatles and Stuart Sutcliffe's mother is writing in England that *he* was the Beatles.

Stu Sutcliffe and John got a flat in Gambia Terrace: I lived rough all right. It was a dirty old flat. I think we spent about four months there, practising and painting. It was just like a rubbish dump. There must have been about seven of us in the same place. It was in a terrible condition. There was no furniture, just beds. And as we were just loafing about, we didn't really think of it as home. The others tried to tidy it up a bit but we didn't bother — except I think I bought a piece of old carpet or something. I left all my gear there when I went to Hamburg.

ON A HAMBURG ROOF TOP.

1960.

ON STAGE AT THE STAR CLUB, HAMBURG.

1960: Hamburg: At first we got a pretty cool reception. Then the manager said we should "Mak Show", like the group down the road were doing. So we tried. We were a bit scared by it all at-first, being in the middle of the tough club land. But we felt cocky, being from Liverpool, at least believing the myth about Liverpool producing cocky people.

The first Mak Show I did was to jump around in one number like Gene Vincent. Every number lasted twenty minutes, just to spin it out. We all did Mak Shoing all the time from then on. We only once ever tried a German number, playing to the crowd. Paul learned "Wooden Heart", which was very popular. We got better and got more confidence. We couldn't help it, with all the experience, playing all night long. It was handy them being foreign. We had to try even harder, put our heart and soul into it, to get ourselves over.

In Liverpool we'd only ever done one-hour sessions and we just used to do our best numbers, the same ones, at every one. In Hamburg we had to play for eight hours, so we really had to find a new way of playing. We played very loud! Bang! Bang! All the time. The Germans loved it.

To get the Germans going and keep it up for 12 hours, we'd really had to hammer. We had to try anything that came into our heads in Hamburg. There was nobody to copy from.

Your voice began to hurt with the pain of singing. We learned from the Germans that you could stay awake by eating slimming pills, so we did that.

We just used to shout in English at the Germans. Call them Nazis and tell them to fuck off.

What with playing, drinking and birds, how could we find time to sleep?

First George, then Paul and Pete were deported from Germany leaving John and Stu stranded: We'd spent our money as we went along. I didn't have any to spare. I felt real sorry for myself. And it was a pretty hungry business working my way back to home. Being stuck in Hamburg with no food money was no joke ... especially just around Christmas.

When I did get home, I was so fed up I didn't bother to contact the others for a couple of weeks. I didn't know what they were doing. Anyway, after a while I got to thinking that we ought to cash in on the Liverpool beat scene. Things were really thriving and it seemed a pity to waste the experience we'd got playing all those hours every night in Hamburg.

Musical Differences: From our earliest days in Liverpool, George and I on the one hand and Paul on the other had different musical tastes.

Paul preferred 'pop type' music and we preferred what is now called 'underground'.

This may have led to arguments, particularly between Paul and George, but the contrast in our tastes, I am sure, did more good than harm, musically speaking, and contributed to our success.

1961.

Mersey Beat. July 6, 1961: BEING A SHORT DIVERSION ON THE DUBIOUS ORIGINS OF BEATLES Translated from the John Lennon
Once upon a time there were three little boys called John, George and Paul, by name christened. They decided to get together because they were the getting together type. When they were together they wondered what for after all, what for? So all of a sudden they all grew guitars and formed a noise. Funnily enough, no one was interested, least of all the three little men. So-o-o-o on discovering a fourth little even littler man called Stuart Sutcliffe running about them they said, quote 'Sonny get a bass guitar and you will be alright' and he did — but he wasn't alright because he couldn't play it. So they sat on him with comfort 'til he could play. Still there was no beat, and a kindly old aged man said, quote 'Thou hast not drums!' We had no drums! they coffed. So a series of drums came and went and came.

Suddenly, in Scotland, touring with Johnny Gentle, the group (called the Beatles called) discovered they had not a very nice sound — because they had no amplifiers. They got some. Many people ask what are Beatles? Why Beatles? Ugh, Beatles, how did the name arrive? So we will tell you. It came in a vision — a man appeared on a flaming pie and said unto them 'From this day on you are Beatles with an A'. Thank you, Mister Man, they said, thanking him.

And then a man with a beard cut off said — will you go to Germany (Hamburg) and play mighty rock for the peasants for money? And we said we would play mighty anything for money.

But before we could go we had to grow a drummer, so we grew one in West Derby in a club called Some Casbah and his trouble was Pete Best. We called 'Hello, Pete, come off to Germany!' 'Yes!' Zooooom. After a few months, Peter and Paul (who is called McArtrey, son of Jim McArtrey, his father) lit a Kino (cinema) and the German police said 'Bad Beatles, you must go home and light your English cinemas'. Zooooom, half a group. But even before this, the Gestapo had taken my friend little George Harrison (of Speke) away because he was only twelve and too young to vote in Germany; but after two months in England he grew eighteen, and the Gestapoes

said 'you can come'. So suddenly all back in Liverpool Village were many groups playing in grey suits and Jim said 'Why have you no grey suits?' 'We don't like them, Jim' we said speaking to Jim. After playing in the clubs a bit, everyone said 'Go to Germany!' So we are. Zooooom. Stuart gone. Zoom zoom John (of Woolton) George (of Speke) Peter and Paul zoom zoom. All of them gone.

Thank you club members, from John and George (what are friends).

'Our best work was never recorded': We were four guys ... I met Paul, and said, "You want to join me band?" Then George joined and then Ringo joined. We were just a band that made it very, very, big that's all. Our best work was never recorded. We were performers in Liverpool, Hamburg and other dance halls. What we generated was fantastic, when we played straight rock, and there was nobody to touch us in Britain. As soon as we made it, we made it, but the edges were knocked off.

You know Brian put us in suits and all that, and we made it very, very big. But we sold out, you know. The music was dead before we even went on the theater tour of Britain. We were feeling shit already, because we had to reduce an hour or two hours' playing, which we were glad about in one way, to 20 minutes, and we would go on and repeat the same 20 minutes every night.

The Beatles music died then, as musicians. That's why we never improved as musicians; we killed ourselves then to make it. And that was the end of it. George and I are more inclined to say that; we always missed the club dates because that's when we were playing music, and then later on we became technically, efficient recording artists — which was another thing — because we were competent people and whatever media you put us in we can produce something worthwhile.

December 3, 1961: The Silver Beatles met Brian Epstein: We were in a daydream till he came along. We'd no idea what we were doing. Seeing our marching orders on paper made it all official. Brian was trying to clean our image up. He said we'd never get past the door of a good place.

He'd tell us that jeans were not particularly smart and could we possibly manage to wear *proper* trousers. But he didn't want us suddenly looking square. He let us have our own sense of individuality. We respected his views. We stopped champing at cheese rolls and jam butties on stage. We paid a lot more attention to what we were doing. Did our best to be on time. And we smartened up, in the sense that we wore suits instead of any sloppy old clothes.

Brian Epstein: Everything is true and not true about everything. I mean, we certainly weren't naive. We were no more naive than he was. I mean, what was he? ... He served in a record shop. So Epstein was serving in a record shop and he had nothing to do, and saw these sort of ... rockers, greasers, playing loud music and *a lot* of kids paying attention to it. And he thought, well "This is a business to be in," and he liked it — he liked the look of it. He wanted to manage us, and he told us that he thought he could manage us and we had nobody better so we said all right, you can do it. Then he went around shopping, getting us work, and it got to a point where he said, "Look, if you cut your hair you'll get this" ... For at that time it was longer than in any of the photographs. It was generally cut or trimmed for the photographs; even in school photographs your hair was cut the day before, or when you had a holiday. Somehow your parents always managed to cut your hair. But there were some private pictures that show it was pretty long for those days, and greased back, hanging around. There was a lot of long hair on the teddy boys ... the Tony Curtises that grew larger and larger because they never went to the hairdresser.

We were pretty greasy. Outside of Liverpool, when we went down South in our leather outfits,

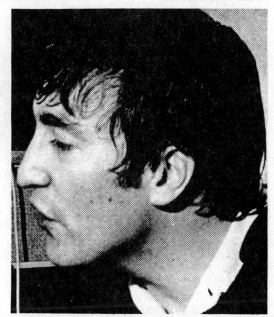

the dance hall promoters didn't really like us. They thought we looked like a gang of thugs. So it got to be like Epstein said, "Look if you wear a suit ....", and everybody wanted a good suit, you know? A nice sharp, black suit man ... We liked the leather and the jeans but we wanted a good suit, even to wear offstage. "Yeah man, I'll have a suit". So if you wear a suit, you'll get this much money ... all right, wear a suit, I'll wear a suit. I'll wear a bloody *balloon* if somebody's going to pay me. I'm not in love with the leather *that* much.

He was our salesman, our front. You'll notice that another quirk of life is — I may have read this somewhere — that self-made men usually have someone with education to front for them, to deal with all the other people with education. Now Epstein had enough education to go in and deal with the hobnobs ... and it's the same thing now. If I have a lawsuit, I have to get a lawyer.

Epstein fronted for the Beatles, and he played a great part of whatever he did. He was theatrical — that was for sure. And he believed in us. But he certainly didn't package us the way they say he packaged us. He was good at his job, but to an extent he wasn't the greatest business-man. He was theatrical and he *believed*. But you have to look at it this way: if he was such a great packager, so clever at packaging products, whatever happened to Gerry and the Pacemakers and all the other packages? Where are they? Where are those packages? Only one package survived, the original package. It was a mutual deal. You want to manage us? Okay, we'll let you. We *allow* you to — we weren't picked up off the street. We allowed him to take us. Paul wasn't that keen, but he's more conservative in the way he approaches things. He even says that himself — and that's all well and good — maybe he'll end up with more yachts.

WITH GENE VINCENT AT THE CAVERN.

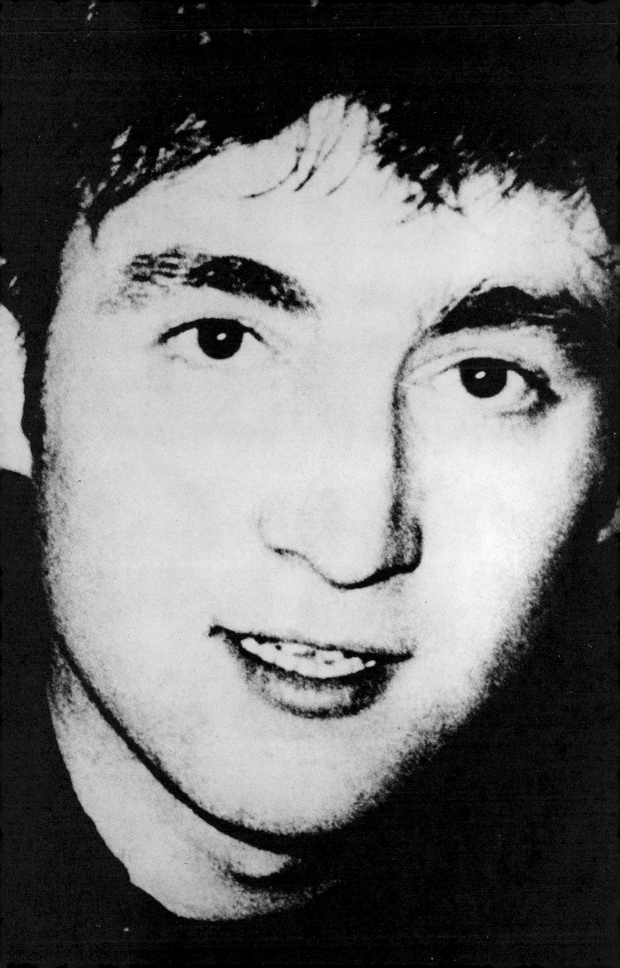

1962.

CYNTHIA LENNON WITH HER HUSBAND.

August 15, 1962: Parlophone Records (EMI) agreed to sign The Beatles and John, Paul and George asked Brian Epstein to fire Pete Best and replace him with Ringo: We were cowards but if we'd told Pete to his face that would have been nastier. It would have probably ended in a fight.

John got Cynthia pregnant: I said, yes, we'll have to get married. I didn't fight it . When I told my Aunt Mimi she just let out a groan.

August 23, 1962: John and Cynthia got married: I couldn't hear a word the bloke was saying for the noise of a drill outside.

I did feel embarrassed. Walking about, married. It was like walking about with odd socks on or your fly open.

The Beatles moved to London: When we came down, we were treated like real provincials by the Londoners. We were in fact, provincials.

That was a great period. We were like kings of the jungle then, and we were very close to the Stones. I don't know how close the others were but I spent a lot of time with Brian and Mick. I admire them, you know. I dug them the first time I saw them in whatever that place is they came from, Richmond. I spent a lot of time with them, and it was great. We all used to just go around London in cars and meet each other and talk about music with the Animals and Eric and all that. It was really a good time, that was the best period, fame-wise. We didn't get mobbed so much. It was like a men's smoking club, just a very good scene.

1963.

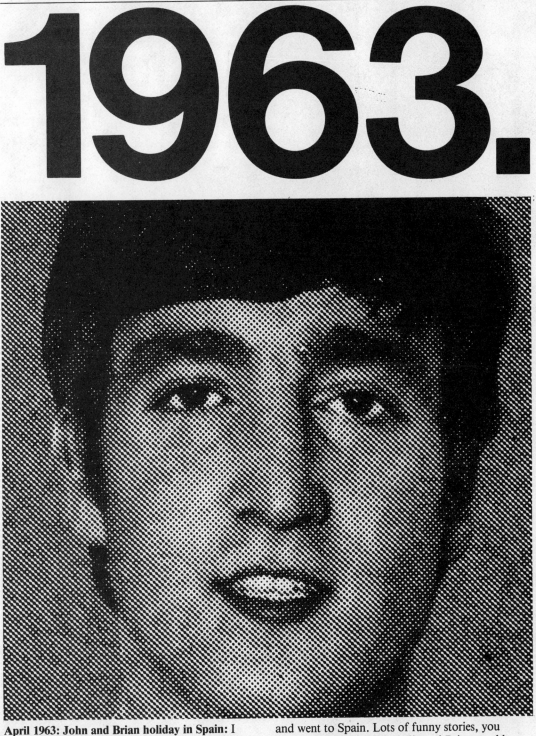

April 1963: John and Brian holiday in Spain: I went on holiday to Spain with Brian — which started all the rumors that he and I were having a love affair, but not quite. It was never consummated. But we did have a pretty intense relationship. And it was my first experience with someone I knew was a homosexual. He admitted it to me. We had this holiday together because Cyn was pregnant and we left her with the baby and went to Spain. Lots of funny stories, you know. We used to sit in cafés and Brian would look at all the boys and I would ask, "Do you like that one? Do you like this one?" It was just the combination of our closeness and the trip that started the rumors.

October 1963: Beatlemania Begins: "Everyone can be a success". If you keep saying that enough

times to yourself, you can be. We are not better than anybody else. What's talent? I don't know. Are you born with it? Do you discover it later on? The basic talent is believing you can do something.

Up to the age of fifteen I was no different from any other little cunt of fifteen. Then I decided I'd write a little song and I did. But it didn't make any difference. That's a load of crap that I discovered a talent. I just did it. I've no talent except a talent for being happy or a talent for skiving.

November 4, 1963: At the Royal Command Variety Performance at the Prince of Wales Theatre in Piccadilly Circus with the Queen Mother and Princess Margaret present...: On this next number I want you all to join in. Would those in the cheap seats clap their hands. The rest of you can rattle your jewellery.

We did manage to refuse all sorts of things that people don't know about. For instance, we did the Royal Variety Show once, and we were asked discreetly to do it every year after that — but we always said 'stuff it'. So every year there was always a story in the newspapers saying: 'Why No Beatles For The Queen,' which was pretty funny, because they didn't know we'd refused it. That show's a bad gig anyway. Everybody's very nervous and uptight and nobody performs well. The time we did do it, I cracked a joke on stage. I was fantastically nervous, but I wanted to say something just to rebel a bit, and that was the best I could do.

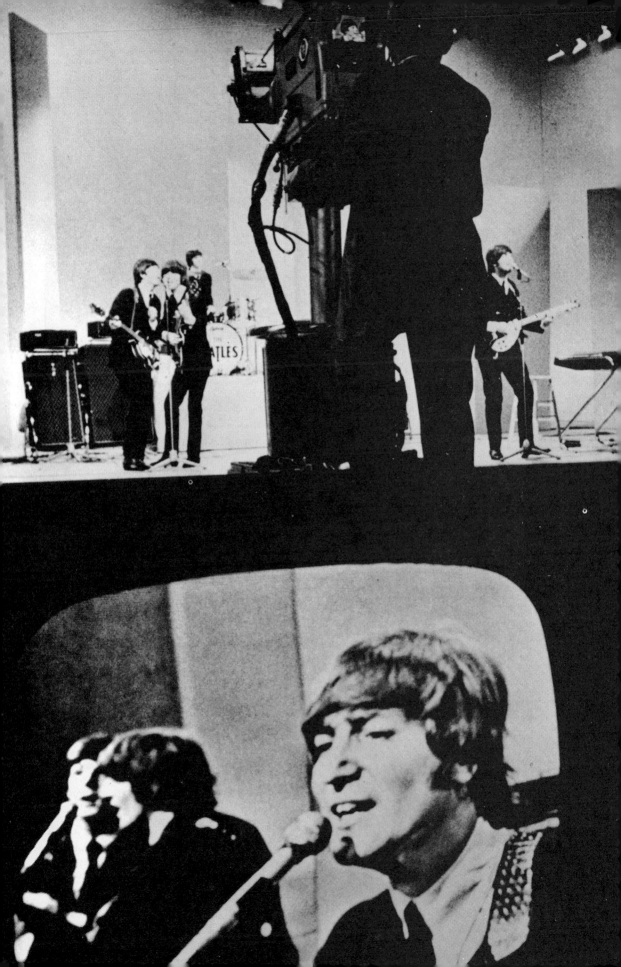

1964.

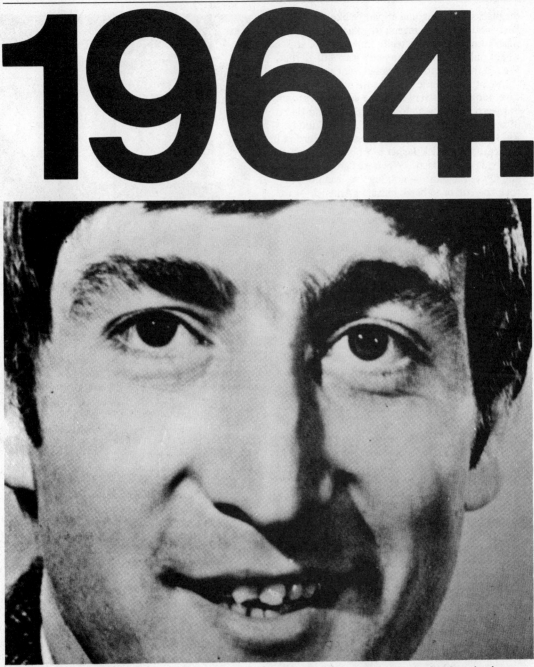

February 7, 1964: First U.S. Tour: We were really professional by the time we got to the States; we had learned the whole game. When we arrived here we knew how to handle the press; the British press were the toughest in the world and we could handle anything. We were all right.

On the plane over, I was thinking "Oh, we won't make it", or I said it on a film or something, but that's that side of me. We knew we would wipe you out if we could just get a grip on you. We were new.

And when we got here, you were all walking around in fuckin' Bermuda shorts, with Boston crew cuts and stuff on your teeth. Now they're telling us, they're all saying, Beatles are *passé* and this is like that, man. The chicks looked like fuckin' 1940 horses. There was no conception of dress or any of that jazz. We just thought "What an ugly race", it looked just disgusting. We thought how hip we were, but, of course, we weren't. It was just the five of us, us and the Stones were really the hip ones; the rest of England were just the same as they ever were.

You tend to get nationalistic, and we would really laugh at America, except for its music. It was the black music we dug, and over here even the blacks were laughing at people like Chuck Berry and the blues singers; the blacks thought it wasn't sharp to dig the really funky music, and the whites only listened to Jan and Dean and all that. We felt that we had the message which was "Listen to this music". It was the same in Liverpool, we felt very exclusive and underground in Liverpool, listening to Richie Barret and Barrett Strong, and all those old-time records. Nobody was listening to any of them except Eric Burdon in Newcastle and Mick Jagger in London. It was that lonely, it was fantastic. When we came over here and it was the same — nobody was listening to rock and roll or to black music in America — we felt as though we were coming to the land of its origin but nobody wanted to know about it.

March 25, 1964: 'In His Own Write' published: I put things down on sheets of paper and stuff them in my pockets. When I have enough, I have a book. I suppose they were all manifestations of hidden cruelties. They were very Alice in Wonderland and Winnie the Pooh. I was very hung-up then. I got rid of a lot of that. It was my version of what was happening then. It was the usual criticisms as some critic put it. If I wrote it in normal spelling there would be no point in writing. I'm not saying anything. There is no message.

In His Own Write: Compared to what I earn from the royalties will be chicken-feed but that's not the important thing. Up to now we've done everything together and this is all my own work. I keep thinking I'm breaking my contract. I first began to write when I was fourteen. Just private stuff for myself and my friends. Then when the group started going on the road I used to take out my typewriter after the show and just tap away as the fancy took me. Then a friend of mine took some of the material to Cape, the publishers, and the

man there said: 'This is brilliant. I'd like to do this.' And that was before he even knew who I was .

A Spaniard in the Works: You know, I was very pleased about the first one. To my amazement the reviewers liked it, and they wouldn't have been biased by the fact I was a Beatle, even if the fans were. To tell you the truth they took the book more seriously than I did myself. It just began as a laugh for me ... at grammar school they put me in for eight O-levels and I failed every one. I was supposed to get art and English language. Maybe I just didn't get down to work in time. If I hadn't got this job I've got now I don't know what I'd have done. But I'd never have been a shop assistant or anything like that. I'd have come down to London, maybe, and been a poet ... maybe when I'm fifty I might even try a novel .

April 1964: 'Hard Day's Night': I dug 'Hard Day's Night' although Alun Owen only came with us for two days before he wrote the script. He invented that word 'grotty' — did you know that? We thought the word was really weird, and George curled up with embarrassment every time he had to say it. But it's part of the language now — you hear society people using it. Amazing.

Songs for 'Hard Day's Night': There were times when we honestly thought we'd never get the time to write all the material. But we managed to get a couple finished while we were in Paris, during our stay at the Olympia. And three more were completed in America, while we were soaking up the sun on Miami Beach.

Drugs To Survive: *A Hard Day's Night* I was on pills, that's drugs, that's bigger drugs than pot. Started on pills when I was 15, no, since I was 17, since I became a musician. the only way to survive

in Hamburg, to play eight hours a night, was to
take pills. The waiters gave you them — the pills
and drink. I was a fucking dropped-down drunk
in art school. *Help* was where we turned on to pot
and we dropped drink, simple as that. I've always
needed a drug to survive. The others, too, but I
always had more, more pills, more of everything
because I'm more crazy probably.

**June 5, 1964: John photographed crawling from
an Amsterdam brothel:** The Beatles tours were like
the Fellini film *Satyricon*. We had that image.
Man, our tours were like something else, if you
could get on our tours, you were in. They were
Satyricon, all right. Wherever we went, there was
always a whole scene going, we had our four
separate bedrooms. We tried to keep them out of
our rooms. Derek's and Neil's rooms were always
full of junk and whores and who-the-fuck-knows-
what, and policemen with it. Satyricon! We had to
do something. What do you do when the pill
doesn't wear off and it's time to go? I used to be
up all night with Derek, whether there was
anybody there or not, I could never sleep, such a
heavy scene it was. They didn't call them groupies
then, they called it something else and if we
couldn't get groupies, we would have whores and
everything, whatever was going.

When we hit town, we hit it. There was no
pissing about. There's photographs of me crawling
about in Amsterdam on my knees coming out of
whore houses and things like that. The police
escorted me to the places, because they never
wanted a big scandal, you see. I don't really want
to talk about it, because it will hurt Yoko. And
it's not fair. Suffice to say, that they were
Satyricon on tour and that's it, because I don't
want to hurt their feelings, or the other people's
girls either. It's just not fair.

The bigger we got, the more unreality we had to
face; the more we were expected to do until, when
you didn't sort of shake hands with a Mayor's
wife, she would start abusing you and screaming
and saying "How dare they?"

There is one of Derek's stories in which we were
asleep after the show in the hotel somewhere in
America, and the Mayor's wife comes and says,
"Get them up, I want to meet them." Derek said,
"I'm not going to wake them." She started to
scream, "You get them up or I'll tell the press."
There was always that — they were always
threatening that they would tell the press about us,
if we didn't see their bloody daughter with braces
on her teeth. It was always the police chief's
daughter or the Lord Mayor's daughter, all the
most obnoxious kids — because they had the most
obnoxious parents — that we were forced to see
all the time. We had these people thrust on us.

The most humiliating experiences were like
sitting with the Mayor of the Bahamas, when we
were making *Help* and being insulted by these

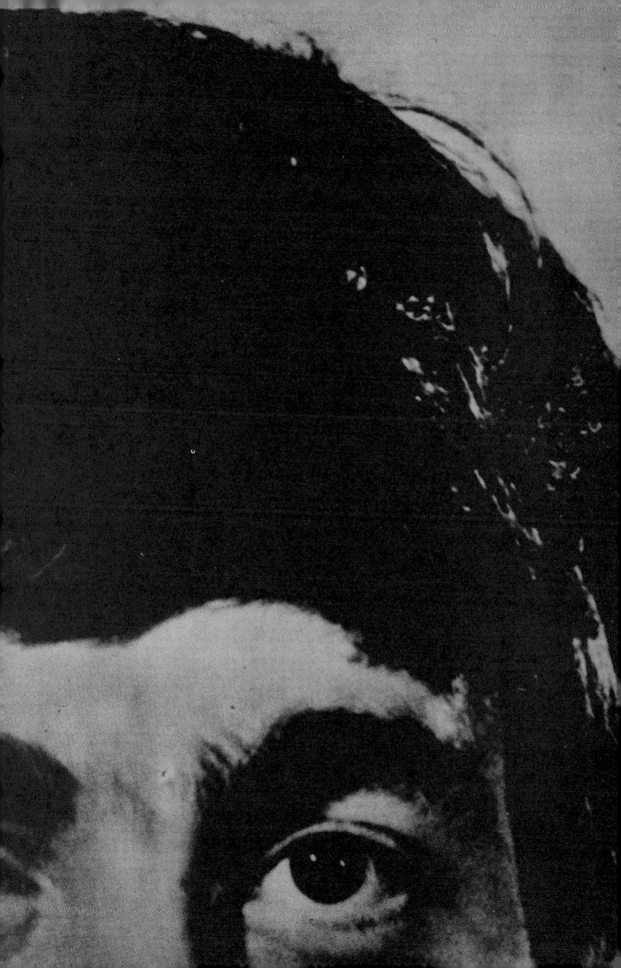

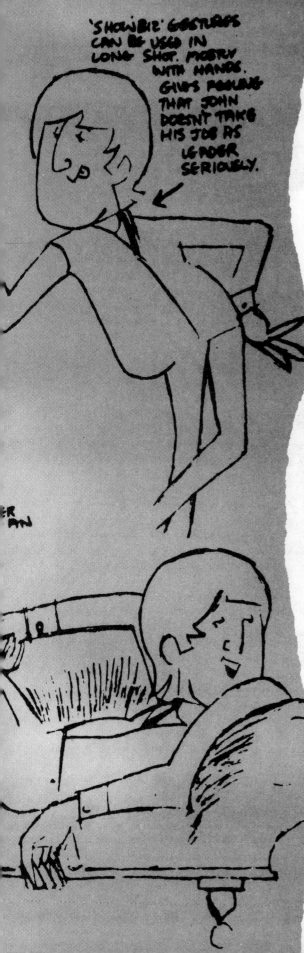

'SHOWBIZ' GESTURES CAN BE USED IN LONG SHOT. MOSTLY WITH HANDS. GIVES FEELING THAT JOHN DOESN'T TAKE HIS JOB AS LEADER SERIOUSLY.

fuckin' junked up middle-class bitches and bastards who would be commenting on our work and commenting on our manners.

All that business was awful, it was a fuckin' humiliation. One has to completely humiliate oneself to be what the Beatles were, and that's what I resent; I didn't know, I didn't foresee. It happened bit by bit, gradually until this complete craziness is surrounding you, and you're doing exactly what you don't want to do with people you can't stand — the people you hated when you were ten.

Fame: Oh sure. I dug the fame, the power, the money, and playing to big crowds. Conquering America was the best thing.

You see we wanted to be bigger than Elvis — that was the main thing.

We reckoned we could make it because there were four of us. None of us would've made it alone, because Paul wasn't quite strong enough, I didn't have enough girl-appeal, George was too quiet, and Ringo was the drummer. But we thought that everyone would be able to dig at least one of us, and that's how it turned out.

Fuckin' big bastards, that's what the Beatles were. You have to be a bastard to make it, that's a fact, and the Beatles are the biggest bastards on earth. Everybody wants the image to carry on. You want to carry on. The press around too, because they want the free drinks and the free whores and the fun; everybody wants to keep on the bandwagon. We were the Caesars; who was going to knock us, when there were a million pounds to be made? All the handouts, the bribery, the police, all the fucking hype. Everybody wanted in, that's why some of them are still trying to cling on to this: don't take Rome from us, not a portable Rome where we can all have our houses and our cars and our lovers and our wives and office girls and parties and drink and drugs, don't take it from us, otherwise you're mad, John, you're crazy, silly John wants to take all this away.

1965.

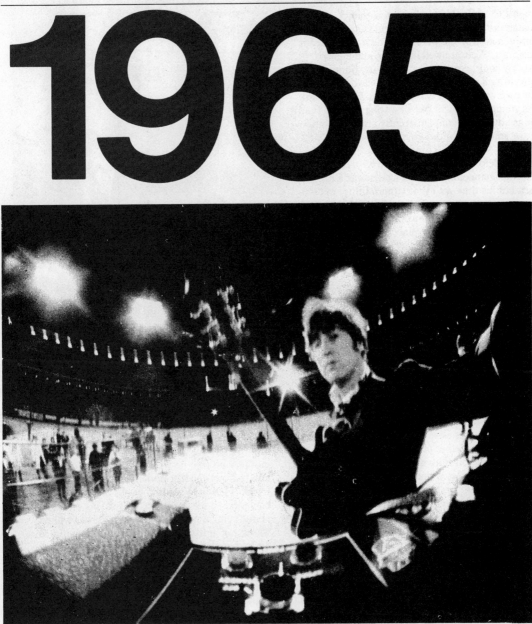

ON STAGE AT SHEA STADIUM

June 12, 1965: Awarded the M.B.E.: In the beginning it was a constant fight between Brian (Epstein) and Paul on one side, and me and George on the other. Brian put us in neat suits and shirts, and Paul was right behind him. I didn't dig that, and I used to try and get George to rebel with me. I'd say to him: 'Look, we don't need these fucking suits. Let's chuck them out of the window.'

My little rebellion was to have my tie loose, with the top button of my shirt undone, but Paul'd always come up to me and put it straight. I saw a film the other night, the first television film we ever did. The Granada people came down to film us, and there we were in suits and everything — it just wasn't us, and watching that film I knew that that was where we started to sell out.

We had to do a lot of selling out then. Taking the MBE was a sell-out for me. You know, before you get an MBE the Palace writes to you to ask if you're going to accept it, because you're not supposed to reject it publicly and they sound you out first. I chucked the letter in with all the fan-mail, until Brian asked me if I had it. He and a few other people persuaded me that it was in our interests to take it, and it was hypocritical of me to accept it. But I'm glad, really, that I did accept it — because it meant that four years later I could use it to make a gesture.

When my envelope arrived marked OHMS I thought I was being called up ... I shall stick it on the wall or make it into a bell.

August 6, 1965: 'Help' album released: The Beatles thing had just gone beyond comprehension. We were smoking marijuana for breakfast. We were well into marijuana and nobody could communicate with us, because we were just all glazed eyes, giggling all the time. In our own world. That was the song, *Help!* I think everything that comes out of a song — even Paul's songs now, which are apparently about nothing — shows something about yourself.

'Help': Help was a drag, because we didn't know what was happening. In fact Lester was a bit ahead of his time with the Batman thing, but we were on pot by then and all the best stuff is on the cutting-room floor, with us breaking up and falling about all over the place.

'Help': When *Help!* came out in '65, I was actually crying out for help. Most people think it's just a fast rock-'n'-roll song. I didn't realize it at the time; I just wrote the song because I was commissioned to write it for the movie. But later, I knew I really was crying out for help. It was my fat Elvis period. You see the movie: He—I—is very fat, very insecure, and he's completely lost himself. And I am singing about when I was so much younger and all the rest, looking back at how easy it was. Now I may be very positive — yes, yes — but I also go through deep depressions where I would like to jump out the window, you know. It becomes easier to deal with as I get older; I don't know whether you learn control or, when you grow up, you calm down a little. Anyway, I was fat and depressed and I *was* crying out for help.

In those days, when the Beatles were depressed, we had this little chant. I would yell out, "Where are we going, fellows?" They would say, "To the top, Johnny," in pseudo-American voices. And I would say, "Where is that, fellows?" And they would say, "To the toppermost of the poppermost." It was some dumb expression from a cheap movie — à la *Blackboard Jungle* — about Liverpool. Johnny was the leader of the gang.

October 26, 1965: John was late for the press conference the day he was awarded the MBE: I set the alarm for eight o'clock and then just lay there. I thought, well, if anyone wants me — they'll phone me. The phone went lots of times, but that's the one I never answer. My own phone didn't go at all. So I just lay there.

I shall keep it in the smallest room in the house — my study.

Dec 31, 1965: John's father, Freddie, releases a record, 'That's My Life': I never saw him until I made a lot of money and he came back.

I opened the *Daily Express* and there he was, washing dishes in a small hotel or something very

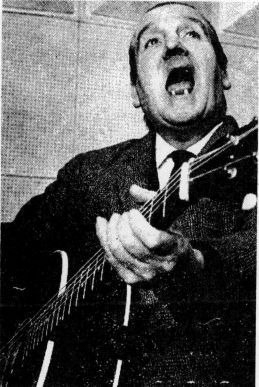

near where I was living in the Stockbroker belt outside London. He had been writing to me to try to get in contact. I didn't want to see him. I was too upset about what he'd done to me and to my mother and that he would turn up when I was rich and famous and not bother turning up before. So I wasn't going to see him at all, but he sort of blackmailed me in the press by saying all this about being a poor man washing dishes while I was living in luxury. I fell for it and saw him and we had some kind of relationship. He died a few years later of cancer. But at 65, he married a secretary who had been working for the Beatles, age 22, and they had a child, which I thought was hopeful for a man who had lived his life as a drunk and almost a Bowery bum.

A lot of us are looking for fathers. Mine was physically not there. Most people's are not there *mentally* and physically, like always at the office or busy with other things. So all these leaders, parking meters, are all substitute fathers, whether they be religious or political.... All this bit about electing a President. We pick our own daddy out of a dog pound of daddies. This is the daddy that looks like the daddy in the commercials. He's got the nice gray hair and the right teeth and the parting's on the right side. OK? This is the daddy we choose. The dog pound of daddies, which is the political arena, gives us a President, then we put him on a platform and start punishing him and screaming at him because Daddy can't do miracles. Daddy doesn't heal us.

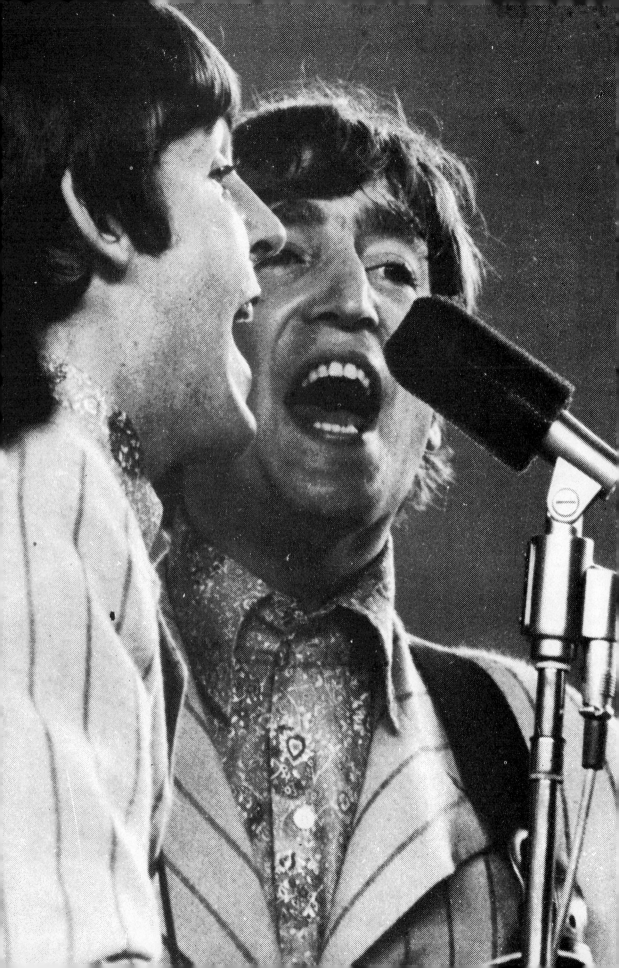

1966.

John and Jesus: March 4, 1966. John Lennon was interviewed by Maureen Cleave in the London *Evening Standard:* Christianity will go. It will vanish and shrink. I needn't argue about that. I'm right and I will be proved right. We're more popular than Jesus now. I don't know which will go first — rock 'n' roll or Christianity. Jesus was all right but his disciples were thick and ordinary. It's them twisting it that ruins it for me.

I can't express myself very well, that's my whole trouble. I was just saying, in my illiterate way of speaking, what I gleaned from Hugh J. Schonfield's book *The Passover Plot*. It was about how Christ's message had been garbled by disciples and twisted for various selfish reasons by those who followed — to the point hwere it lost validity for many today. Actually, if I am going to blame anyone, it's myself for not thinking what people a million miles away were going to say about it. I've just had a reshuffling of all the things pushed into my head. I'm more of a Christian than I ever was. I don't go along with organised relition and the way it has come about. I believe in God, but not as one thing, not as an old man in the sky. I believe that what people call God is something in all of us. I believe that what Jesus and Mohammed and Buddha and all the rest said was right. It's just that the translations have gone wrong.

Jesus says one thing and then all the clubs formed telling their versions and the whole thing gets twisted. It's like a game of having six people in a line and I whisper something to the guy next to me, maybe "love thy neighbour" or "everything ought to be equal". By the time it gets to the end of the line it's altogether something else.

At school, for me religion was normal Church of England, Sunday School and Sunday church. But there was actually nothing going on in the church I went to. Nothing really touched us. Then I was an atheist. And then came The Beatles. We've been mushroom-grown, forced to grow up a bit quick like having thirty-forty-year-old heads on twenty-year-old bodies. We have to develop more sides, more attitudes. If you're a bus-man, you usually have a bus-man's attitude. But we had

to be more than four mop-heads up on a stage. We had to grow up or we'd have been swamped. And so I apologised. It was through being committed to things outside myself. If I were at the same stage I was five years ago, I'd have shouted that we'll never tour again and packed myself off and that would be the end of it. Lord knows, I don't need the money. But when they started burning our records ... that was the real shock, the physical burning. I couldn't go away knowing that I'd created another little piece of hate in the world. Especially with something as uncomplicated as people listening to records and dancing and playing and enjoying what The Beatles are. Not when I could do something about it. If I said tomorrow I'm not going to play again, I still couldn't live in a place with somebody hating me for something irrational.

But that's the trouble with being truthful. You try to apply truth talk, although you have to be false sometimes because the whole thing is false in a way, like a game. But you hope sometime that if you're truthful with somebody they'll stop all the plastic reaction and be truthful back and it'll be worth it. Yet everybody is playing the game and sometimes I'm left naked and truthful with everybody biting me. It's disappointing.

1966: American Tour: On our last tour people kept bringing blind, crippled and deformed children into our dressing room and this boy's mother would say "Go on, kiss him, maybe you'll bring back his sight". We're not cruel. We've seen enough tragedy in Merseyside but when a mother shrieks "Just touch him and maybe he will walk again" we want to run, cry, empty our pockets. We're going to remain normal if it kills us.

November 1966: John met Yoko Ono: How did I meet Yoko? There was a sort of underground clique in London. John Dunbar, who was married to Marianne Faithful, had an art gallery in London called Indica and I'd been going around to galleries a bit on my off days in between records. I'd been to see a Takis exhibition, I don't know if you know what that means, he does multiple electro-magnetic sculptures, and a few exhibitions in different galleries who showed these

sort of unknown artists or underground artists. I got the word that this amazing woman was putting on a show next week and there was going to be something about people in bags, in black bags, and it was going to be a bit of a happening and all that. So I went down to a preview of the show, I go there the night before it opened. I went in — she didn't know who I was or anything — I was wandering around, there was a couple of artsy type students that had been helping lying around there in the gallery, and I was looking at it and I was astounded. There was an apple on sale there for 200 quid, I thought it was fantastic — I got the humor in her work immediately. I didn't have to sort of have much knowledge about avant garde or underground art, but the humor got me straight away. There was a fresh apple on a stand, this was before Apple — and it was 200 quid to watch the apple decompose. But there was another piece which really decided me for-or-against the artist, a ladder which led to a painting which was hung on the ceiling. It looked like a blank canvas with a chain with a spy glass hanging on the end of it. This was near the door when you went in. I

climbed the ladder, you look through the spyglass and in tiny little letters it says "yes".

So it was positive. I felt relieved. It's a great relief when you get up the ladder and you look through the spyglass and it doesn't say "no" or "fuck you" or something, it said "yes".

I was very impressed and John Dunbar sort of introduced us — neither of us knew who the hell we were, she didn't know who I was, she'd only heard of Ringo I think, it means apple in Japanese. And she came up and handed me a card which said "Breathe" on it, one of her instructions, so I just went (pant). That was our meeting.

1967.

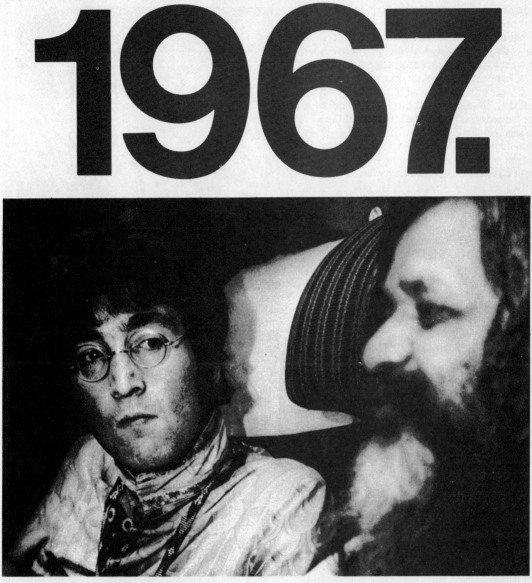

ON THE TRAIN TO BANGOR WITH MAHARISHI.

August 1967: Maharishi Mahesh Yogi: Bangor was incredible, you know. Maharishi reckons the message will get through if we can put it across. What he says about life and the universe is the same message that Jesus, Buddha and Krishna and all the big boys were putting over. Mick came up there and he got a sniff and he was on the phone saying: send Keith, send Brian, send them all down. You just get a sniff and you're hooked.

There's none of this sitting in the lotus position or standing on your head. You just do it as long as you like. (In a heavy accent) Tventy minutes a day is prescribed for ze verkers. Tventy minutes in the morning and tventy minutes after verk. Makes you happy, intelligent and more energy. I mean look how it all started. I believe he just landed in Hawaii in his nightshirt, all on his own, nobody with him, in 1958.

The main thing is not to think about the future or the past, the main thing is just to get on with *now*. We want to help people do that with these academies. We'll make a donation and we'll ask for money from anyone we know with money, anyone that's interested, anyone in the so-called establishment who's worried about kids going wild and drugs and all that. Another groovy thing: everybody gives one week's wages when they join. I think it's the fairest thing I've ever heard of. And that's all you ever pay, just the once.

Even if you go into the meditation bit just curious or cynical, once you go into it, you see. We weren't so much sceptical because we'd been through that phase in the middle of all the Beatlemania like, so we came out of being sceptics a bit. But you've still got to have a questioning attitude to all that goes on. The only thing you can do is judge on your own experience and that's what this is about.

Maharishi was a father figure, Elvis Presley might have been a father figure. I don't know. Robert Mitchum. Any male image is a father figure. There's nothing wrong with it until you give them the right to give you sort of a recipe for your life. What happens is somebody comes along with a good piece of truth. Instead of the truth's being looked at, the person who brought it is looked at. The messenger is worshipped, instead of the message. So there would be Christianity, Mohammedanism, Buddhism, Confucianism, Marxism, Maoism — everything — it is always about a person and never about what he says.

August 27, 1967: Brian dies: We were in Wales with the Maharishi. We had just gone down after seeing his lecture first night. We heard it then, and then we went right off into the Maharishi thing.

We were just outside a lecture hall with Maharishi and I don't know ... I can't remember, it just sort of came over. Somebody came up to us ... the press were there, because we had gone down with this strange Indian, and they said "Brian's dead" and I was stunned, we all were, I suppose, and the Maharishi, we went in to him. "What, he's dead," and all that, and he was sort of saying oh, forget it, be happy, like an idiot, like parents, smile, that's what the Maharishi said. And we did.

I had the feeling that anybody has when somebody close to them dies: there is a sort of little hysterical, sort of hee, hee, I'm glad it's not me or something in it, the funny feeling when somebody close to you dies. I don't know whether you've had it, but I've had a lot of people die around me and the other feeling is, "What the fuck? What can I do?"

I knew we were in trouble then. I didn't really have any misconceptions about our ability to do anything other than play music and I was scared. I thought, "We've fuckin' had it".

I liked Brian and I had a very close relationship with him for years, because I'm not gonna have some stranger runnin' things, that's all. I like to work with friends. I was the closest with Brian, as close as you can get to somebody who lives a sort of "fag" life, and you don't really know what they're doin' on the side. But in the group, I was closest to him and I did like him.

He had great qualities and he was good fun. He had a flair. He was a theatrical man, rather than a businessman. When he got Cilla Black, his great delight was to dress her and present her. He would have made a great dress designer, 'cause that's what he was made for. With us he was a bit like that. I mean, he literally fuckin' cleaned us up and there were great fights between him and me over me not wanting to dress up. In fact, he and Paul had some kind of collusion to keep me straight because I kept spoilin' the image.

We had complete faith in him when he was

runnin' us. To us, he was the expert. I mean originally he had a shop. Anybody who's got a shop must be all right. He went around smarmin' and charmin' everybody. He had hellish tempers and fits and lock-outs and y'know he'd vanish for days. He'd come to a crisis every now and then and the whole business would fuckin' stop 'cause he'd ben on sleepin' pills for days on end and wouldn't wake up. Or he'd be missin' y'know, beaten up by some old docker down the Old Kent Road. But we weren't too aware of it. It was later on we started findin' out about those things.

We'd never have made it without him and *vice versa*. Brian contributed as much as us in the early days, although we were the talent and he was the hustler. He wasn't strong enough to overbear us. Brian could never make us do what we really didn't want to do.

After Brian's Death: With Brian dying it was sort of a big thing for us. And if we hadn't had this meditation it would have been much harder to assess and carry on and know how we were going.

Now we're our managers, now we have to make all the decisions. We've always had full responsibility for what we did, but we still had a father figure, or whatever it was, and if we didn't feel like it — well, you know, Brian would do it. Now we've got to work out all our business, everything, and maybe a lot more to do with NEMS and all the things that Brian left behind. It threw me quite a bit. But then the Maharishi talked to us and, I don't know, cooled us out a bit.

You know, I feel I can handle anything at the moment and I never felt like that before. You know, I've had good days, bad days, periods when things are going right, but I mean this is a

bad period for us in the material sense, in the physical sense. But the greatest period in an inner sense.

September 1967: Magical Mystery Tour: Paul made an attempt to carry on as if Brian hadn't died by saying, "Now, now, boys, we're going to make a record." Being the kind of person I am, I thought well, were going to make a record all right, so I'll go along, so we went and made a record. And that's when we made *Magical Mystery Tour*. That was the real...

Paul had a tendency to come along and say well

he's written these ten songs, let's record now. And I said, "Well, give us a few days, and I'll knock a few off," or something like that. *Magical Mystery Tour* was something he had worked out with Mal and he showed me what his idea was and this is how it went, it went around like this, the story and how he had it all ... the production and everything.

Paul said, "Well, here's the segment, you write a little piece for that," and I thought "Bloody Hell," so I ran off and I wrote the dream sequence for the fat woman and all the thing with the spaghetti. Then George and I were sort of

66

grumbling about the fuckin' movie and we thought we better do it and we had the feeling that we owed it to the public to do these things.

While recording 'Magical Mystery Tour': Ain't no ethnic bastard gonna get no golden castles outta me!

The continuing story of John and Yoko: The second time I met her was at a gallery opening of Claes Oldenberg in London. We were very shy, we sort of nodded at each other and we didn't know — she was standing behind me, I sort of looked away because I'm very shy with people, especially chicks. We just sort of smiled and stood frozen together in this cocktail party thing.

The next thing was she came to me to get some backing — like all the bastard underground do — for a show she was doing. She gave me her Grapefruit book and I used to read it and sometimes I'd get very annoyed by it; it would say things like "paint until you drop dead" or "bleed" and then sometimes I'd be very enlightened by it and I went through all the changes that people go through with her work — sometimes I'd have it by the bed and I'd open it

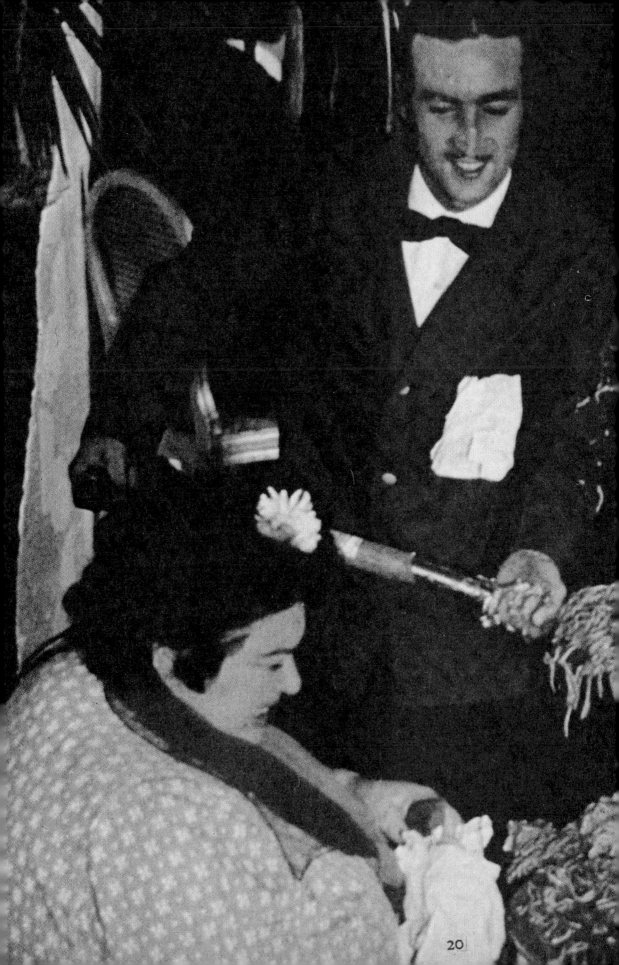

and it would say something nice and it would be alright and then it would say something heavy and I wouldn't like it. There was all that and then she came to me to get some backing for a show and it was half a wind show. I gave her the money to back it and the show was, this was in a place called Lisson Gallery, another one of those underground places. For this whole show everything was in half: there was half a bed, half a room, half of everything, all beautifully cut in half and all painted white. And I said to her "why don't you sell the other half in bottles?" having caught on by then what the game was and she did that — this is still before we'd had any nuptials — and we still have the bottles from the show, it's my first. It was presented as "Yoko Plus Me" — that was our first public appearance. I didn't even go to see the show, I was too up tight.

The beginnings of the breakup: The Beatles broke up after Brian died; we made the double album, the set. It's like if you took each track off it and made it all mine and all George's. It's like I told you many times, it was just me and a backing group, Paul and a backing group, and I enjoyed it. We broke up then.

December 4, 1967: Apple Boutique Opened: Clive Epstein, or some other such business freak, came up to us and said you've got to spend so much money, or the tax will take you. We were thinking of opening a chain of retail clothes shops or some balmy thing like that ... and we were all thinking that if we are going to have to open a shop, let's open something we're interested in, and we went through all these different ideas about this, that and the other. Paul had a nice idea about opening up white houses, where we would sell white china, and things like that, everything white, because you can never get anything white, you know, which was pretty groovy, and it didn't end up with that, it ended up with Apple and all this junk and The Fool and all those stupid clothes and all that.

John began to fall in love with Yoko: It was beginning to happen; I would start looking at her book and that but I wasn't quite aware what was happening to me and then she did a thing called Dance Event where different cards kept coming through the door everyday saying "Breathe" and "Dance" and "Watch all the lights until dawn", and they upset me or made me happy depending on how I felt.

I'd get very upset about it being intellectual or all fucking avant garde, then I'd like it and then I wouldn't. Then I went to India with the Maharoonie and we were corresponding. The letters were still formal but they just had a little side to them. I nearly took her to India as I said but I still wasn't sure for what reason, I was still sort of kidding myself, with sort of artistic reasons, and all that.

1968.

IN INDIA WITH THE MAHARISHI.

March 1968: The Beatles leave the Maharishi in India and return to England: There was a big hullaballo about him trying to rape Mia Farrow or somebody and trying to get off with a few other women and things like that. We went to see him, after we stayed up all night discussing was it true or not true. When George started thinking it might be true, I thought well, it must be true; because if George started thinking it might be true, there must be something in it.

So we went to see Maharishi, the whole gang of us, the next day, charged down to his hut, his bungalow, his very rich-looking bungalow in the mountains, and as usual, when the dirty work came, I was the spokesman — whenever the dirty work came, I actually had to be leader, wherever the scene was, when it came to the nitty gritty, I had to do the speaking — and I said, "We're leaving."

"Why?" he asked, and all that shit and I said, "Well, if you're so *cosmic*, you'll know why."

He was always intimating, and there were all these right-hand men always intimating, that he did miracles. And I said, "You know why," and he said, "I don't know why, you must tell me," and I just kept saying "You ought to know" and he gave me a look like, "I'll kill you, you bastard," and he gave me such a look. I knew then. I had called his bluff and I was a bit rough to him.

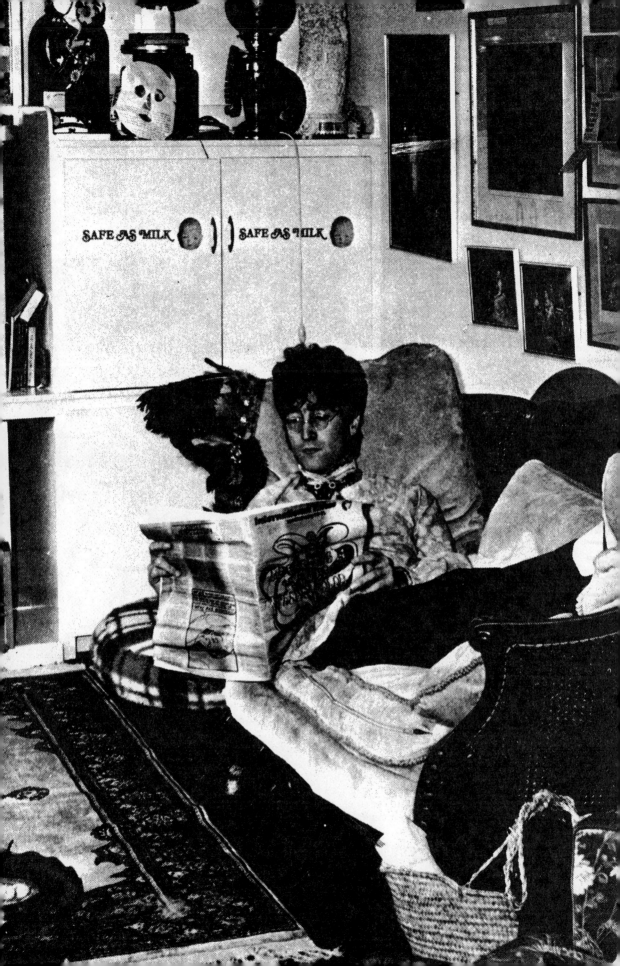

May 15, 1968: John and Paul launched Apple Records in New York: The aim of the company isn't a stack of gold teeth in the bank. We've done that bit. It's more of a trick to see if we can get artistic freedom within a business structure; to see if we can create things and sell them without charging three times our cost.

Apple was a manifestation of Beatle naivety, collective naivety. We said, "We're going to do this and help everybody" and all that and we got conned on the subtlest and bluntest level. We really didn't get approached by the best artists, we got all the bums from everywhere else. All the ones that everyone had thrown out. The ones who were really groovy wouldn't approach us because they were too proud. We had to quickly build up another wall round us to protect us from all the beggars and lepers in Britain and American who came to see us. Our lives were getting insane! I tried when we were in Wigmore Street (*Apple's original offices*), to see everyone like we said, everyone day in and day out, and there wasn't anyone who had anything to offer to society or me or anything. There was just, "I want, I want, and why not?" and terrible scenes like that going on in the offices with different spades and hippies and all different people very wild with me. Even on the peace campaign we had a lot of that too. Once you open the door it's hard you know.

October 1968: John announces his love for Yoko: I've never known love like this before, and it hit me so hard that I had to halt my marriage to Cyn. And don't think that was a reckless decision, because I felt very deeply about it and all the implications that would be involved. When we are free — and we hope that will be within a year — we shall marry. There is no need to marry — as Mick and Marianne say — but there's nothing lost in marrying either.

Some may say my decision was selfish. Well, I don't think it is. Are your children going to thank you when they are eighteen? There is something else to consider, too — isn't it better to avoid rearing children in the atmosphere of a strained relationship?

My marriage to Cyn was not unhappy. But it was just a normal marital state where nothing happened and which we continued to sustain. You sustain it until you meet someone who suddenly sets you alight.

With Yoko I really knew love for the first time. Our first attraction was a mental one, but it happened physically too. Both are essential in the union — but I never thought I would marry again. *Now the thought of it seems so easy.*

When we got back from India we were talking to each other on the phone. I called her over, it was the middle of the night and Cyn was away, and I thought well now's the time if I'm gonna get to know her anymore. She came to the housle and I didn't know what to do; so we went upstairs to my studio and I played her all the tapes that I'd made, all this far out stuff, some comedy stuff, and some electronic music. She was suitably impressed and then she said well let's make one ourselves so we made "Two Virgins". It was midnight when we started "Two Virgins," it was dawn when we finished, and then we made love at dawn. It was very beautiful.

October 18, 1968: John and Yoko busted: So all of a sudden like, there is this knock on the door and a woman's voice outside and I look around and there is this policeman standing in the window wanting to be let in. We'd been in bed and our (he made a mock prudish face) lower regions were uncovered, like. Yoko ran into the bathroom to get dressed with her head poking out so they wouldn't think she was hiding anything. And then I said: "Ring the lawyer, quick," but she went and rang Apple, I'll never know why. So then they got us for obstruction which was ridiculous because we only wanted to get our clothes on.

The press are outraged at John for loving Yoko and being arrested for drugs: I've blown my top, isn't that the word? That my thinking has gone wrong and all the things I've got into have put me in disgrace. If I am to believe that — what should I do? Send my MBE back to the Queen? Is that what they want?

November 9, 1968: 'Two Virgins' released: The main hangup in the world today is hypocrisy and insecurity. If people can't face up to the fact of other people being naked or smoking pot, or whatever they want to do, then we're never going to get anywhere. People have got to become aware that it's none of their business and that being nude is not obscene. Being ourselves is what's important. If everyone practised being themselves instead of pretending to be what they aren't, there would be peace.

'Two Virgins': We were both a bit embarrassed when we peeled off for the picture — so I took it myself with a delayed action shutter.

The picture was to prove that we are not a couple of demented freaks, that we are not deformed in any way and that our minds are healthy. If we can make society accept these kind of things without offence, without sniggering then we shall be achieving our purpose. There has got to be law and order, but that doesn't mean we should suffer bad, out-of-date laws. If laws weren't changing they would still be jumping on queers and putting them away.

So there is a case for us all to put society right — and that is basically why there is unrest all over the world; because a revolution must come.

A is for Parrot which we can plainly see.

B is for glasses which we can plainly see.

C is for plastic which we can plainly see

D is for Doris

E is for binoculars I'll get it in five

F is for Ethel who lives next door

G is for Orange which we love to eat when we can get them because they come from abroad.

H is for England and (Heather)

I is for monkey we see in the tree

J is for parrot which we can plainly see.

K is for shoetop we wear to the ball

L is for lamo because brown

M is for Venezuela where the oranges come from

N is for Brazil near Venezuela (very near)

O is for football which we kick about a bit

T is for Tommy who won the war

Q is a garden which we can plainly see

R is for intestines which hurt when we dance

S is for pancake or whole wheat bread

U is for Ethel who lives on the hill

P is arab and her sister will

V is for we

W is for lighter which never lights

X is easter – have one yourself

Y is a crooked letter and you can't straighten it

Z is for Apple which we can plainly see.

This is my story both humble and true
take it to pieces and mend it with glue.

John Lennon 1969. Feb.

1969.

PHOTO BY PAUL McCARTNEY.

The other Beatles object to Yoko Ono: They insulted her and they still do...they don't even know I can see it, and even when it's written down it will look like I'm just paranoid, or she's paranoid, I know. Just by the way the publicity on us was handled in Apple all of the two years we were together, and the attitude of people to us and the bits we hear from the office girls. We know, so they can go stuff themselves...(Paul) said many times that at first he hated Yoko and then got to like her. It's too late for me, I'm for Yoko, you know. Why should she take that kind of shit from those people. They were writing about her looking miserable in "Let It Be". You sit through sixty sessions with the most big-headed, uptight people on earth and see what it's fuckin' like, and be insulted by, just because you love someone. And George, shit, insulted her right to her face in the Apple office at the beginning; just being "straight forward" you know, that game of "Well, I'm going to be upfront because this is what we've heard, and Dylan, and a few people said she'd got a lousy name in New York, and you gave off bad vibes." That's what George said to her and we both sat through it, and I didn't hit him, I don't know why, but I was always hoping that they would come around. I couldn't believe it, you know. And they all sat there with their wives, like a fucking jury, and judged us...Ringo was all right, so was Maureen, but the others really gave it to us. I'll never forgive them...although I can't help still loving them either.

77

Heroin: It just was not too much fun. I never injected it or anything. We sniffed a little when we were in real pain. We got such a hard time from everyone, and I've had so much thrown at me, and at Yoko, especially at Yoko. Like Peter Brown in our office — and you can put this in — after we come in after six months he comes down and shakes my hand and doesn't even say hello to her. That's going on all the time. And we get into so much pain that we have to do something about it. And that's what happened to us. We took "H" because of what the Beatles and others were doing to us. But we got out of it.

ALLEN KLEIN

February 3, 1969: Allen Klein appointed Beatles manager: It's really marvellous. People were very scared of him to start with — and some still are — but that's probably good. He's swept out all the rubbish and the deadwood, and stopped it being a rest-house for all the world's hippies. He won't let people order antique furniture for their offices and so forth, he's really tightened it up and it's starting to work a lot better. He noticed that the Beatles had stopped selling records as they were doing around the world, and he found out that it was because the record company simply wasn't bothering to push them. They thought that our records would sell themselves, and they were wrong. They don't.

It you can get to number one in Turkey, Greece, Switzerland, and a couple of other countries then that's as good financially as getting a number one in Britain — they don't realise that. Klein's very good — he's going to make sure they stop sitting on the records and actually release them. He's even keeping tabs on me — I usually make mistakes about who to get in to survey my house, and I can spend a fortune without getting anything done. He's making sure that I do it the right way.

I wanted him as my manager. I introduced him to the other three. But if Paul is trying to suggest that I was rushing them and pushing them down

their throats, this is a wrong impression.

I thought that Paul would agree with us in the end after he had seen the benefit of Klein's work. I would have liked him to have agreed with us before the ABKCO agreement was signed, but I thought he was being unreasonable towards the other three of us, and knew that in the last resort his signature was not necessary.

So far as I am concerned Paul did accept Klein as the Beatles manager, though he may not have liked him.

Paul's criticisms of Klein may reflect his dislike of the man but I don't think they are fair. Klein is certainly forceful to an extreme but he does get results. He doesn't sow discord, between us.

Royalties are coming in in greater sums than they ever were before Klein started to re-organise the Beatles' affairs.

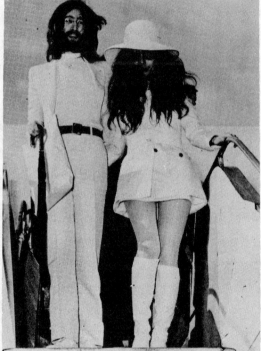

ARRIVAL IN GIBRALTAR.

March 20, 1969: John and Yoko get married: I let Paul McCartney go first — a sort of dry run. Then we began trying to fix something quiet up. We got married in Gibraltar because we tried to get married everywhere else first. I set out to get married on the car ferry and we would have arrived in France married. But they wouldn't do it. We were no more successful with cruise ships. We tried embassies. But three weeks' residence in Germany, or two weeks in France, was required. Gibraltar was a bit small for us to move about for a honeymoon. The wedding was quiet and British.

Intellectually, we knew marriage was a stupid scene, but we're romantic and square as well as hip and aware. We lived together for a year before we got married but we were still tied to other people by a bit of paper. One day some guy came in and said here's your divorce papers, you're free, and the release was like a burden we didn't know we were carrying. Now, the point is we want to bind ourselves together in all the ways possible, so we got a new set of papers, and if there are any more ceremonies, we'll go through them. When we got the new certificate, we were very emotional about it...Yoko was crying.

March 26, 1969: First 'Bed Peace' held at Amsterdam Hilton: It was a nice high. We were on the seventh floor of the Hilton looking over Amsterdam — it was very crazy, the press came expecting to see us fucking in bed — they all heard John and Yoko were going to fuck in front of the

press for peace. So when they all walked in — about 50 or 60 reporters flew over from London all sort of very edgy, and we were just sitting in pyjamas saying "Peace Brother", and that was it. On the peace thing there's lots of heavy discussions with intellectuals about how you should do it and how you shouldn't.

Our life is our art. That's what the bed-ins were. When we got married, we knew our honeymoon was going to be public, anyway, so we decided to use it to make a statement. We sat in bed and talked to reporters for seven days. It was hilarious. In effect, we were doing a commercial for peace on the front page of the papers instead of a commercial for war.

Second Thoughts on 'Bed Peace': I have to admit that some of my early political activities with Yoko were pretty naive. But Yoko was always political in an avant garde kind of way. She had this idea that you must always make use of newspaper publicity to get across the idea of peace. Any excuse, such as our wedding, was enough...

She believed that you should make people laugh, too. The trouble with Rubin and Hoffman was that they never wanted laughter...they wanted violence. I've never been into violence myself, although I'm aware sometimes of violence inside me. I have a violent nature. Perhaps that's why I like New York.

All you need is love, like the songs says. That's really my ultimate political belief. We all need more love. But I found that being political interfered with my music. I'm still a musician first, not a politician. At 34 my greatest fear and dread is that I may become *bored* with music. You see, I believe that music is not peripheral to society, but a necessity to it. I don't believe that musicians are parasites.

BED PEACE IN AMSTERDAM.

May 26, 1969: Second "Bed Peace" held at the Queen Elizabeth Hotel, Montreal, Canada, to run for ten days: We think students are being conned by the establishment. The establishment is like the school bully. It aggravates you and aggravates you until you hit it. And then they'll kill you. That's how they're playing it now. They're testing people!

You gotta remember, establishment, it's just a name for — evil. The monster doesn't care whether it kills all the students or whether there's a revolution. It's not thinking logically, it's out of control, it's suffering from, it's a careless killer and it doesn't care whether the students all get killed or black power — it'll enjoy that. Whatever the rabbit or the sheep does, it doesn't matter, the cat is playing with it. And whether the rabbit gets away a few hundred yards, it doesn't matter, they'll get it. We've got to realize that it doesn't care which way we go. But the only thing it can't fight is the mind. But the students have got conned into thinking that they can change it with violence.

It doesn't make sense because the monster's insane. The blue meanie is insane. We're the only ones that really care about life. To them it doesn't matter. Destruction is good enough for them. It's not just the government, it's power or the devil or whatever we call it. It doesn't matter to him. Either way he gets his kicks. And his kicks are control or destruction. If he can't control, he destroys. We're the only ones interested in life, the peaceniks or whatever. We've got to make the others aware of it — the ones, the borderline ones who don't know.

Evil, the same thing that's caused it for millions of years. Evil is a way of life. We've got to get through, we've got to get past that. We want to live.

OK, the Russians had their revolution and it was for the same reasons, oppression, poverty and all that — and look at Russia now. Every time you have a violent revolution, the guns reign, you shoot the others — that's if they don't get you — and you get power. But you'll have to build the structures that have been wrecked and once you build things up again, you build a new establishment and you're back in the same bag. Don't think that because the black cause is different from the Jewish cause, or the communist

cause is different from the capitalistic cause, that it's going to be any different. It's going to be the same game. You smash it down, you build it up, then you have to hold on to it. And the people who hold on to it are the ones who usually carry the gun.

We think all of this is wrong. Violence begets violence, it's a universal law. All right, some will say situations vary from place to place and the situation will sometimes justify the use of violence, but that's a compromise and I say peace cannot be compromised. If you're sitting on the beach and the water's there, there are always people who will say it's too deep, there's too much current and too

many sharks. Well, it might be silly, but we're for diving in the water to learn how to swim; it's the only way. The establishment likes to infiltrate war games. They like to make you think the only way is violence. Show me a violent revolution that brought about peace and freedom, then I'd say OK you're right. For two million years, we've had violence...so what's wrong with trying out peace for a change?

If there is a cart going along the road there, dropping a load of crap there, we can either run after the cart and sweep it up, which is what some people do, and that's OK. Or you can try to catch up with driver and tell him to stop, you know, and that is what we are trying to do.

I think the youth have picked up the Establishment paranoia. Like it was Make Love, Not War a few years ago. It's turned into KILL THE PIGS. The whole place is paranoic and I want to remind them; REMEMBER LUV. Remember that you have love inside you and so has the pig. Give Peace a chance...Kiss A Cop For Peace Week!

September 13, 1969: On the flight to Toronto to play at the Rock & Roll Festival: I said to Paul, "I'm leaving". I knew on the flight over to Toronto or before we went to Toronto: I told

Allen I was leaving, I told Eric Clapton and Klaus that I was leaving then, but that I would probably like to use them as a group. I hadn't decided how to do it — to have a permanent new group or what — then later on, I thought fuck, I'm not going to get stuck with another set of people, whoever they are.

I announced it to myself and the people around me on the way to Toronto a few days before. And on the plane — Klein came with me — I told Allen, "It's over". When I got back, there were a few meetings, and Allen said well, cool it, cool it, there was a lot to do, business-wise you know, and it would not have been suitable at the time.

RECORDING 'LET IT BE'.

CONCERT AT THE LYCEUM, LONDON.

Then we were discussing something in the office with Paul, and Paul said something or other about the Beatles doing something, and I kept saying "No, no no," to everything he said. So it came to a point where I had to say something, of course, and Paul said, "What do you mean?"

I said, "I mean the group is over, I'm leaving."

Allen was saying don't tell. He didn't want me to tell Paul even. So I said, "It's out." I couldn't stop it, it came out. Paul and Allen both said that they were glad that I wasn't going to announce it, that I wasn't going to make an event out of it. I don't know whether Paul said don't tell anybody, but he was darned pleased that I wasn't going to. He said, "Oh, that means nothing really happened if you're not going to say anything."

So that's what happened. So, like anybody when you say divorce, their face goes all sorts of colours. It's like he knew really that this was the final thing; and six months later he comes out with whatever. I was a fool not to do it, not to do what Paul did, which was use it to sell a record.

September 30, 1969: 'Cold Turkey' recorded:
When I wrote it I went to the other three Beatles and said "Hey lads, I think I've written a new single." But they all said 'Ummmm...arrrr...welll' because it was going to be my project, and so I thought "Bugger you I'll put it out myself." That had happened once before, when I was wanting to put 'Revolution' out as a single, but 'Hey Jude' went out instead.

November 25, 1969: Your Majesty,
I am returning my MBE in protest against Britain's involvement in the Nigeria-Biafra thing, against our support of America in Vietnam and against 'Cold Turkey' slipping down the charts. With love,
John Lennon

1970.

THE RELEASE OF JOHN'S & YOKO'S FIRST SOLO ALBUMS.

April 1970: the rumours of the Beatles breakup became too strong to be denied: If the Beatles or the Sixties had a message, it was to learn to swim. Period. And once you learn to swim, swim. The people who are hung up on the Beatles' and the Sixties' dream missed the whole point when the Beatles' and the Sixties' dream *became* the point. Carrying the Beatles' or the Sixties' dream around all your life is like carrying the Second World War and Glenn Miller around. That's not to say you can't enjoy Glenn Miller or the Beatles, but to live in that dream is the twilight zone. It's not living now. It's an illusion.

The Beatles, you see — I'm too involved in them artistically. I cannot see them objectively. I cannot listen to them objectively. I'm dissatisfied with every record the Beatles ever fucking made. There ain't *one* of them I wouldn't remake — including all the Beatles records and all my individual ones. So I cannot possibly give you an assessment of what the Beatles are.

When I was a Beatle, I thought we were the best fucking group in the god-damned world. And believing that is what made us what we were — whether we call it the best rock 'n' roll group or the best pop group or whatever.

But you play me those tracks today and I want to remake every damn one of them. There's not a single one...I heard *Lucy in the Sky with Diamonds* on the radio last night. It's *abysmal*, you know. The track is just *terrible*. I mean, it's great, but it wasn't made right, know what I mean? But that's the artistic trip, isn't it? That's why you keep going. But to get back to your original question about the Beatles and their music, the answer is that we did some good stuff and we did some bad stuff.

When I first got out of the Beatles I thought: "Oh great, I don't have to listen to Paul and Ringo and George". But it's boring yodelling by yourself in a studio. I was always waiting for a reason to get out of The Beatles from the day I filmed 'How I Won The War'. I just didn't have the guts to do it.

The seed was planted when the Beatles stopped touring, and I couldn't deal with not going on stage. But I was too frightened to step out of the palace. That's what killed Presley. Whatever made the Beatles, the Beatles also made the Sixties the Sixties.

Anybody who thinks that if John and Paul got together with George and Ringo, the Beatles would exist is out of their skulls. The Beatles gave everything they had to give, and more. The four guys who used to be that group can never be that group again, even if they wanted to be.

What if Paul and I got together? It would be boring. Whether George and Ringo joined in would be irrelevant, because Paul and I created the music, okay? But going back to the Beatles would be like going back to school...I was never one for reunions. It's all over!

ARRIVING FOR THE PREMIERE OF 'IN HIS OWN WRITE'.

April-May 1970: John and Yoko undertake Primal Therapy in Los Angeles: Janov showed me how to feel my own fear and pain, therefore I can handle it better than I could before, that's all. I'm the same, only there's a channel. It doesn't just remain in me, it goes round and out. I can move a little easier.

I still think that Janov's therapy is great, you know, but I don't want to make it into a big Maharishi thing. If people know what I've been through there, and if they want to find out, they can find out, otherwise it turns into *that* again.

I don't think anything else would work on me. But then of course, I'm not *through* with it; it's a process that is going on. We primal almost daily. You *see*, I don't really want to get this big Primal thing going because it is so embarrassing. The thing in a nutshell: primal therapy allowed us to feel feelings continually, and those feelings usually make you cry. That's all. Because before, I wasn't feeling things, that's all. I was blocking the feelings, and when the feelings come through, you cry. It's as simple as that, really.

December 11, 1970: "JOHN LENNON/PLASTIC ONO BAND" released: Anybody that sings with a guitar and sings about something heavy would tend to sound like this. I'm bound to be influenced by those, because that is the only kind of real *folk* music I really listen to. I never liked the fruity Judy Collins and Baez and all of that stuff. So the only folk music I know is about miners up in Newcastle, or Dylan. In that way I would be influenced, but it doesn't sound like Dylan to me.

I put "fucking" in because it fit. I didn't even realize that there were *two* in the song until somebody pointed it out. When I actually sang it, I missed a verse which I had to add in later. You do say "fucking crazy"; that is how I speak. I was very near to it many times in the past, but, I would deliberately *not* put it in, which is the real hypocrisy, the real stupidity.

I was watching TV as usual, in California, and there was this old horror movie on, and the bells sounded like that to me. It was probably different, because those were actually bells slowed down that they used on the album. They just sounded like that and I thought oh, that's how to start 'Mother.' I knew 'Mother' was going to be the first track so...Actually I wrote 'Mother' in England, 'Isolation' in England and a few more. I finished them off in California. You will have to push me if you want more detail. 'Look At Me' was written around the Beatles' double album time, you know, I just never got it going, there are a few like that lying around.

Well, like a lot of the words, it just came out of me mouth. 'God' was put together from three

songs almost. I had the idea that "God is the concept by which we measure pain," so that when you have a word like that, you just sit down and sing the first tune that comes into your head and the tune is simple, because I like that kind of music and then I just rolled into it. It was just going on in my head and I got by the first three or four, the rest just came out. Whatever came out.

I don't know when I realized that I was putting down all these things I didn't believe in. So I could have gone on, it was like a Christmas card list: where do I end? Churchill? Hoover? I thought I had to stop. I was going to leave a gap, and just fill in your own words: whoever you don't believe in. It had just got out of hand, and Beatles was the final thing because I no longer believe in myth, and Beatles is another myth.

I don't believe in it. The dream is over. I'm not just talking about the Beatles, I'm talking about the generation thing. It's over, and we gotta — I have to personally — get down to so-called reality.

December 31, 1970: McCartney filed suit to break up The Beatles partnership: When Brian died, Apple was full of hustlers and spongers. The staff came and went as they pleased and were lavish with money and hospitality. We have since discovered that at around that time two of Apple's cars had completely disappeared and also that we owned a house which no-one can remember buying.

People were robbing us and living on us to the tune of...18 or 20 thousand pounds a week, was rolling out of Apple and nobody was doing anything about it. All our buddies that worked for us for fifty years, were all just living and drinking and eating like fuckin' Rome, and I suddenly realized it and said we're losing money at such a rate that we would have been broke, really broke. We didn't have anything in the bank really, none of us did. Paul and I could have probably floated, but we were sinking fast. It was just hell, and it had to stop.

1971.

May 1971: The Political Views of John Lennon:
I've always been politically minded, you know, and against the status quo. It's pretty basic when you're brought up, like I was, to hate and fear the police as a natural enemy and to despise the army as something that takes everybody away and leaves them dead somewhere, I mean, it's just a basic working class thing, though it begins to wear off when you get older, get a family and get swallowed up in the system. In my case I've never not been political, though religion tended to overshadow it in my acid days; that would be around '65 and '66. And that religion was directly the result of all that superstar shit — religion was an outlet for my repression. I thought, "Well, there's something else to life, isn't there? This isn't it, surely?" But I was always political in a way, you know. In the two books I wrote, even though they were written in a sort of Joycean gobbledygook, there's many knocks at religion

and there is a play about a worker and a capitalist.
I've been satirizing the system since my childhood.
I used to write magazines in school and hand them
around. I was very conscious of class, they would
say with a chip on my shoulder, because I knew
what happened to me and I knew about the class
repression coming down on us — it was a fucking
fact but in the hurricane Beatle world it got left
out — I got farther away from reality for a time.

At the time it was thought that the workers had
broken through, but I realize in retrospect that it's
the same phoney deal they give to blacks, it was
just like they allowed blacks to be runners or
boxers or entertainers. That's the choice they
allow you — now the outlet is being a pop star,
which is really what I'm saying in Working Class
Hero. As I told Rolling Stone, it's the same people
who have power, the class system didn't change
one little bit. Of course there are a lot of people
walking around with long hair now and some
trendy middle class kids in pretty clothes. But
nothing changed except that we all dressed up a
bit, leaving the same bastards running everything.

Even during the Beatle heyday I tried to go
against it, so did George. We went to America a
few times and Epstein always tried to waffle on at
us about saying nothing about Vietnam. So there
came a time when George and I said "Listen,
when they ask next time, we're going to say that
we don't like that war and we think they should
get right out." That's what we did. At that time

'SAVE OZ' DEMO, LONDON.

this was a pretty radical thing to do, especially for "Fab Four." It was the first opportunity I personally took to wave the flag a bit. But you've got to remember that I'd always felt repressed. We were all so pressurized that there was hardly any chance of expressing ourselves, especially working at that rate, touring continually and always kept in a cocoon of myths and dreams. It's pretty hard when you are Ceasar and everyone is saying how wonderful you are and they are giving you all the goodies and the girls, it's pretty hard to break out of that to say, "Well, I won't want to be king, I want to be real." So in its way the second political thing I did was to say "The Beatles are bigger than Jesus". That really broke the scene. I nearly got shot in America for that. It was a big trauma for all the kids that were following us. Up to then there was this unspoken policy of not answering delicate questions, though I always read the papers, you know, the political bits. The continual awareness of what was going on made me feel ashamed I wasn't saying anything. I burst out because I could no longer play that game any more, it was just too much for me. Of course, going to America increased the build up on me, especially as the war was going on there. In a way we'd turned out to be a Trojan Horse. The Fab Four moved right to the top and then sang about drugs and sex and then I got more and more into the heavy stuff and that's when they started dropping us.

When I started, Rock and Roll itself was the basic revolution to people of my age and situation. We needed something loud and clear to break through all the unfeeling and repression that had been coming down on us kids. We were a bit conscious to begin with of being imitation Americans. But we delved into music and found that it was half white Country-and-Western and half black rhythm and blues. Most of the songs came from Europe and Africa and now they were coming back to us. Many of Dylan's best songs came from Scotland, Ireland, and England. It was a sort of cultural exchange. Though I must say the more interesting songs to me were the black ones because they were more simple. They sort of said shake your arse or your prick which was an innovation really. And then there were the field sons, mainly expressing the pain they were in. They couldn't express themselves intellectually so they had to say in a very few words what was happening to them. And then there was the City blues and a lot of that was about sex and fighting. A lot of this was self-expression but only in the last few years have they expressed themselves completely with Black Power, like Edwin Starr making War records. Before that many black singers were still labouring under that problem of God, it was often, "God will save us." But right through the blacks were singing about their pain and also about sex, which is why I like it.

October 7, 1971: 'Imagine' released: 'Imagine' was a sincere statement. It was 'Working Class Hero' with chocolate on. I was trying to think of it in terms of children.

We recorded it at home in our studio, Phil Spector produced it, and George Harrison plays on about four or five of the tracks and he does some mother solos, especially on one of them. Nicky Hopkins plays piano on the album and he's great. Jim Gordon, Andy Weiser and Jim Keltner are also on it. It's a lighter and happier album than the last, and I've tentatively titled it *Imagine* which is the title of one of the songs. Yoko wrote one of the tracks, something called 'Oh My Love's Very Beautiful', and she designed the album.

'Imagine', both the song itself and the album, is the same thing as 'Working Class Hero' and 'Mother' and 'God' on the first disc. But the first record was too real for people, so nobody bought it. It was banned on the radio. But the song 'Imagine', which says: "Imagine that there was no more religion, no more country, no more politics" is virtually the communist manifesto, even though I am not particularly a communist and I do not belong to any movement. You see, 'Imagine' was exactly the same message, but sugar-coated. Now 'Imagine' is a big hit almost everywhere — anti-religious, anti-nationalistic, anti-conventiona, anti-capitalistic song, but because it is sugar-coated it is accepted. Now I understand what you have to do. Put your political message across with a little honey. This is what we do above all, Jerry, Yoko and the others, it is to try to change the apathy of young people. The apathy which exists in America but which is infiltrating everywhere because everyone follows the American pattern, above all because of the music. The life style of this century has been fashioned by America. Young people are apathetic. They think there is nothing worthwhile to do and everything is finished. They want to

take refuge in drugs to destroy themselves our work is to tell them that there is still hope and still a lot to do. We have to change their minds; we have to tell them that it is OK. Things can change, and just because flower-power did not work it doesn't mean that everything is finished. It is only the beginning. The revolution has only just begun. It is just the beginning of big changes.

The track 'How Do You Sleep' caused great controversy: You know, I wasn't really feeling that vicious at the time. But I was using my resentment toward Paul to create a song, let's put it that way. He saw that it pointedly refers to him, and people kept hounding him about it. But, you know, there were a few digs on *his* album before mine. He's so obscure other people didn't notice them, but I heard them. I thought, Well, I'm not obscure, I just get right down to the nitty-gritty. So he'd done it his way and I did it mine. But as to the line you quoted, yeah, I think Paul died creatively, in a way.

August 1971: John and Yoko moved to New York City: If I'd lived in Roman times, I'd have lived in Rome. Where else? Today America is the Roman Empire and New York is Rome itself.

Before, when I was a Beatle, I was a kind of prisoner in this city. We were always being driven around in cars, between hotels and studios, but we never got see anything or to *know* it at all. Even without my "green card" I'm not as much a prisoner now as I was then. Being a Beatle, living in that incredible fish-tank, matured us in some ways, but not in others. We used to meet Heads of State, but we never got to see reality, whatever reality is.

Yoko and I were for ever coming and going to New York, so finally we decided it would be cheaper and more functional to actually live here. We began in the West Village, the quiet part, and then we moved into a posh apartment overlooking the park on Central Park West. That's still my official residence. Yoko still lives there.

It was Yoko who sold me on New York. She'd been poor here and she knew every inch. She made me walk around the streets and parks and squares and examine every nook and cranny. In fact, you could say that I fell in love with New York on a street corner...And I still do that with newcomers today, drop them down outside the Plaza and make them walk through Central Park, down to the East River, the Hudson, everywhere.

I think for me it has to do with Liverpool. There's the same quality of energy, of vitality, in both cities. New York is at my speed. It's a 24-hours-a-day city, it's going on around you all the time, so much so that you almost stop noticing it. But it's all there if you want it: the telephone can bring you anything and everything. I like to finish work here in the studio at 4 a.m. and go out

and find it all still throbbing.

I think I've graduated in a way: from Liverpool to London and from London to New York. I behave here as I've behaved all my life, you know. I lead a quiet life really, I don't go out to eat more than once or twice a week. Friends fly in from London sometimes and ask where's the action and I have to ring another friend to find out...

I know there are rough areas in New York, but I don't visit them often. The district can change abruptly within one block, but I find I can walk the streets quite freely. People recognise me, but they don't trouble me too much. Sometimes they want to audition right there on the street, which can be a bit embarrassing. But they don't recognise me so much since I shaved my beard off. I shaved it off because I was finding it difficult to eat.

The cab-drivers here are something else, they treat me almost as one of the locals. The younger, hippy types still regard me as a rock super-star — they're always turning right round to ask questions and terrifying me.

I like New Yorkers because they have no time for the niceties of life. They're like me in this. They're naturally aggressive, they don't believe in wasting time.

After I left Liverpool I never looked upon anywhere else as being my home. It was always just wherever I was living at that particular time. Here in New York everything is much faster...with more traffic, more people, more nationalities, more of everything. It must be how London was maybe eighty or a hundred years ago in Victorian days. It's bustin' like crazy and when you're here you feel it with the result that it either wears you

out or you go right along with it. I used to have the same thing with London compared to Liverpool, 'cause in a way it was the same kinda change and I now have the same feeling about New York City.

Not only was Yoko educated here but she also spent 15 years living in New York, so, as far as I was concerned, it was just like returning to your wife's home town...a second home. She knows so much about this place that it quickly broke the ice for me.

No matter where you go, nowhere's anywhere unless you know someone to visit or a restaurant in which to eat in. Y'know, there's nothing lonelier than London when you first arrive there and it's the same here. Though I'm really groovin' on it now, I won't really know how I feel about New York until I've lived here a few years.

June 6, 1971: Lennon met Zappa and jammed with him at the Fillimore: I don't know why I should have believed it because I should know better, having had all that guff written about me, but I expected sort of a grubby maniac with naked women all over the place, you know — sitting on the toilet. The first thing I said was, "Wow, you look so different. You look great!" And he said, "You look clean too"...he was a expecting a couple of nude freaks.

June 6, 1971: John appeared on Howard Smith's WPLJ talk show: *Caller:* Hello?
John: (German accent) This is WFBI, playing all your favourite toons.
Caller: Hello?
John: This Edgar Hoover here and I'd like to do your room.
Caller: You'd like to do my room? What colour would you like to paint it?
John: No, no. I'm gonna *Hoover* it, Ha, ha, haw! *Mother!*

1972.

September 15, 1972: 'Sometime In NYC' released: Life's too short and suddenly you're thirty, and there's all these things going on in the world, and there's so much to do that you never got around to doing because you were doing whatever it was people expected of you. The point, now, is that I want to say whatever it is I've got to say, as simple as the music I like. And that's rock 'n' roll — and to match the lyrics to the music. So now it's...A — WOP BOP-A-LOO-BOP, Get Outta Ireland. I suppose it looks more preachy than it really is. I call it artistic. But it's no more or less than any other artist who may be expressing himself, whether it's with paints or with music.

Most other people express themselves by shouting or playing football at the weekend. But me, here am I in New York and I hear about the thirteen people shot dead in Ireland, and I react immediately. And being what I am, I react in four-to-the bar with a guitar break in the middle. I don't say "My God what's happening...we should do something".

I go: "It was Sunday Bloody Sunday and they shot the people down." It's not like the Bible. It's all over now. It's gone. It's finished. There is no more. My songs are not there to be digested and pulled apart like the Mona Lisa.

When we made that album, we weren't setting out to make the Brandenburg Concerto or the masterpiece everyone always tries to write, paint,

IN GREENWICH VILLAGE LOFT

draw or film. There was no intention of that. It was just a question of getting it done; putting it out and the next one's coming up soon. We needn't have done it. We could have sat on 'Imagine' for a year and a half. But the things on 'New York City' were coming outta our minds, and we just wanted to share our thoughts with anybody who wanted to listen. It was a quicker decision to make 'Sometime In New York City' than any other album. And for that reason it only took nine days to complete.

November 1972: I could not put on the flashy white suit, the lipstick, shout "C'mon everybody!" and play at being Elvis or Mick Jagger, because I honestly don't think I could pull it off even if I tried. Music for me is the only thing worth doing or communicating. Most other things — like who you are, what you wear, and how the lighting is placed — only tend to interfere. If the music's OK, what the hell does it matter what else is going on? It's all secondary. It gets in the way. The whole glamour scream-thing — it'll always be with us. People jumped on the Beatles and screamed in the same way they're now jumping all over T-Rex. It's what supposed to happen. At the beginning it's very encouraging, sure. And being the non-cynical old cynic I was in those days, I could enjoy having one foot in the King's Court. The trouble is some people feel the screaming has to go on happening all the time. Get to that stage and it quickly becomes uninteresting.

RECORDING 'SOMETIME ...'

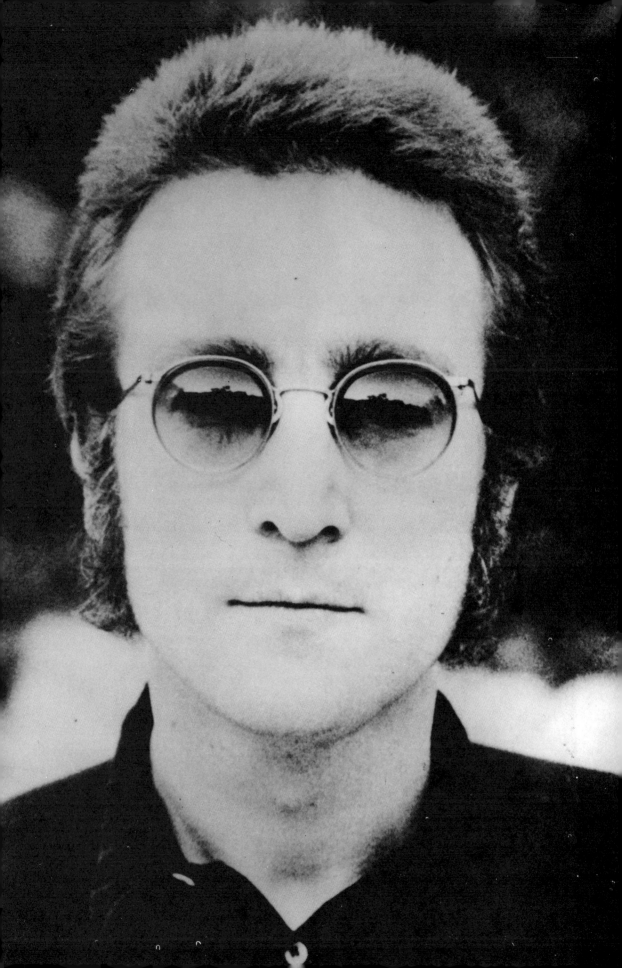

1973.

1973: Moved to Los Angeles to work on 'Rock and Roll' with Phil Spector and separated from Yoko: It started in '73 with Phil and fell apart. I ended up as part of mad drunk scenes in Los Angeles and I finally finished it off on me own. And there was still problems with it up to the minute it came out. I can't begin to say, it's just *barmy*, there's a jinx on that album.

1974: Los Angeles: Now LA, that's a different pace, a different life-style altogether. New York and LA, they have a kind of Manchester/Liverpool thing going. People out there are sensitive about their city too, but I find it bland and I don't like the smog.

In LA you either have to be down by the beach or you become part of that never-ending show-business party circuit. That scene makes me nervous and when I get nervous I have to have a drink and when I drink I get aggressive. So I prefer to stay in New York. I try not to drink at all here.

A drunken evening at The Troubadour in Los Angeles with Harry Nilsson: I picked up a Kotex in a restuarant, in the toilet, and it was clean and just for a gag I came back to the table with it on me head. And 'cause it stuck there with sweat, just *stayed* there, I didn't have to keep it on. It just stayed there till it fell off. And the waitress said, "Yeah, you're an asshole with a Kotex on," and I think it's a good remark and so what? It was my first night on Brandy Alexanders and my last. And I was with Harry Nilsson who was no help at all.

Ask any rockstar about lawsuits. And the more money there is, the more lawsuits there are, the bigger the artist, the more lawsuits. I mean, people sue me for anything; that bloody fan with the Instamatic who sued me for hitting her. I never touched her, never went near the girl — in the Troubadour, the famous Troubadour incident.

She sued me, and I had to pay her off to shut her up. That happens all the time, she just wanted money. People sue you if you bump into them on the street. I do admit to chasing some weird people around, but she was not in the scene...

Well, I was not in the best frame of mind, and I was wildly drunk. But I was nowhere near this chick, she's got no photographs of me near her. It was my first night on Brandy Alexanders, and they tasted like milkshakes. The first thing I knew I was out of me gourd.

Of course Harry Nilsson was no help feeding them to me, saying "Go ahead John". It is true I was wildly obnoxious, but I definitely didn't hit this woman who just wanted to get her name in the papers and a few dollars.

1974.

WITH NILSSON AND 'PUSSY CATS' COVER.

1974: John produced Harry Nilsson's 'Pussy Cats' album: I go in to produce the guy, expecting to hear Harry Nilsson singing and the guy has no voice. We'd committed studio time and we did one track, virtually, and that's the end of his voice. So them I'm stuck with one of the best white singers in America — with no voice at all. Harry didn't tell me till nearly the end of the album that he was coughin' up *blood*.

I didn't know 'cause he *always* looked so wiped out. I didn't know what it was. I was always treatin' him like a doctor, gettin' him to bed at night and tellin' him, you know, don't drink, don't smoke, etcetera, etcetera. Don't do any stuff, man. Not only have you got no voice but they're gonna blame me. Which they did. I think it was psychosomatic. I think he was nervous 'cause *I* was producing him. You know, he was an old Beatle fan when he was in the *bank* or something. But I was committed to the thing, the band was there and the guy had no voice, so we made the best of it. So they say, oh, he's tryin' to sound like you. The poor guy couldn't get a note out and we were lucky to get anything out of it.

October 4, 1974: 'Walls And Bridges' released: Let's say this last year has been an extraordinary year for me personally. And I'm almost amazed that I could get *anything* out. But I enjoyed doing

Walls and Bridges and it wasn't hard when I had the whole thing to go into the studio and do it. I'm surprised it wasn't just all *bluuuuugggggghhhh*. I had the most peculiar year. And...I'm just glad that *something* came out. It's describing the year, in a way, but it's not as sort of schizophrenic as the year really was. I think I got such a shock during that year that the impact hasn't come through It isn't all on *Walls and Bridges* though. There's a hint of it there. It has to do with age and God knows what else. But only the surface has been touched on *Walls and Bridges*, you know?

Musically, my mind was just a clutter. It was apparent on 'Walls And Bridges', which was the work of a semi-sick craftsman. There was no inspiration and it gave an aura of misery...I became an artist because I cherished freedom — I couldn't fit into a classroom or office. I wasn't free at all. I've withdrawn many times. Part of me was a monk, and part a performing flea. I found out life doesn't end when you stop subscribing to Billboard.

1974: John and Yoko live apart for 18 months: Yoko and I are still very good friends. I still love her, but we're two artists and we found it hard living together. We talk on the phone every day, whether she's in Britain or here.

105

1975.

IN THE DAKOTA, OVERLOOKING CENTRAL PARK.

February 1975: Beatles lawsuit finally settled: In a nutshell, what was arranged was that everybody get their own individual monies. Even up till this year — till the settlement was signed — all the monies were going into one pot. All individual records, mine, Ringo's, Paul's — all into one big pot. It had to go through this big machinery and then come out to us, eventually. So now, even on the old Beatle royalties, everything goes into four separate accounts instead of one big pot all the time. That's that. The rest of it was ground rules. Everybody said the Beatles've signed this paper, that means they're no longer tied in any way. That's bullshit. We still own this thing called Apple. Which, you can explain, is a *bank*. A bank the money goes into. But there's still the entity itself known as Beatles. The product, the name, the likeness, the Apple thing itself, which still exists, and we still have to communicate on it and make decisions on it and decide who's to run Apple and who's to do what. It's not as cut and dried as the papers said.

Mid 1975: John and Yoko got back together: It's not a matter of *who* broke it up. *It* broke up. And why did we end up back together? We ended up together again because it was diplomatically viable...come on. We got back together because we *love* each other. *The separation didn't work out.* That's it. It *didn't* work out. And the reaction to the breakup was all that madness. I was like a chicken without a head.

As a friend says, I went out for coffee and some papers and I didn't come back. (*chuckles*) Or vice versa. It's always written *that* way, y'know. All of us. You know, the *guy* walked. It's never that simple.

It started, somehow, at the end of '73, goin' to do this *Rock 'n' Roll* album. It had quite a lot to do with Yoko and I, whether I knew it or not, and then suddenly I was out on me own. Next thing I'd be waking up drunk in strange places, or reading about meself in the paper, doin' extraordinary things, half of which I'd done and half of which I hadn't done. But you know the game anyway. And find meself sort of in a mad *dream* for a year. I'd been in many mad dreams, but this...It was pretty wild. And then I tried to recover from that.

Meanwhile life was going on, the Beatles settlement was going on, other things, life was still going on and it wouldn't let you sit with your hangover, in whatever form that took. It was like something — probably meself — kept hitting me while I was trying to do something. I was still trying to carry on a normal life and the whip never let up — for eight months. So...that's what was going on. Incidents: You can put it down to which night with which bottle or which night in which town. It was just sort of a mad year like that...And it was just probably fear, and being out on me own, and gettin' old, and are ye gonna make it in the charts? Are ye not gonna make it?

All that crap, y'know. All the garbage that y'really know is not the be-all and end-all of your life, but if other things are goin' funny, *that's* gonna hit you. If you're gonna feel sorry for yourself, you're gonna feel sorry for everything. What it's really to do with is probably the same thing that it's always been to do with all your life; whatever your own personal problems really are, you know? So it was a year that manifested itself *in most peculiar fashion.* But I'm *through* it and it's '75 now and I feel *better* and I'm sittin' *here* and not lyin' in some weird place with a hang-over. I feel like I've been on Sinbad's voyage, you know, and I've battled all those monsters and I've got back. Weird.

1975: "Alive in '75": I don't want to grow up but I'm sick of not growing up — that way. I'll find a different way of not growing up. There's a better way of doing it than torturing your body. And then your mind. The guilt! It's just so *dumb*. And it makes me *furious* to be dumb because I don't like dumb people. And there I am, doing the dumbest things...I seem to do the things that I despise the most, almost. All of that to — what? — avoid being normal.

I have this great fear of this *normal* thing. You know, the ones that passed their exams, the ones that went to their jobs, the ones that didn't become rock & roller, the ones that settled for it, settled for it, settled for the *deal*! That's what I'm trying to avoid. But I'm sick of avoiding it with violence, you know? I've gotta do it some other way. I think I will. I think just the fact that I've realized it is a good step forward. Alive in '75 is my new motto. I've just made it up. That's the one. I've decided I want to live. I'd decided I wanted to live *before*, but I didn't know what it meant, really. It's taken however many years and I want to have a *go* at it.

1975: John retired from public life to become a house-husband: We got back together, decided this was our life, that having a baby was important to us and that anything else was subsidiary to that. We worked hard for that child. We went through all hell trying to have a baby, through many miscarriages and other problems. He is what they call a love child in truth. Doctors told us we could never have a child. We almost gave up. "Well, that's it, then, we can't have one..." We were told something was wrong with my sperm, that I abused myself so much in my youth that there was no chance. Yoko was 43, and so they said, no way. She has had too many miscarriages and when she was a young girl, there were no pills, so there were lots of abortions and miscarriages; her stomach must be like Kew Gardens in London. No way. But this Chinese acupuncturist in San Francisco said, "You behave yourself. No drugs, eat well, no drink. You have child in 18 months." And we said, "But the English doctors said..." He said, "Forget what they said. You have child." We had Sean and sent the acupuncturist a Polaroid of him before he died, God rest his soul.

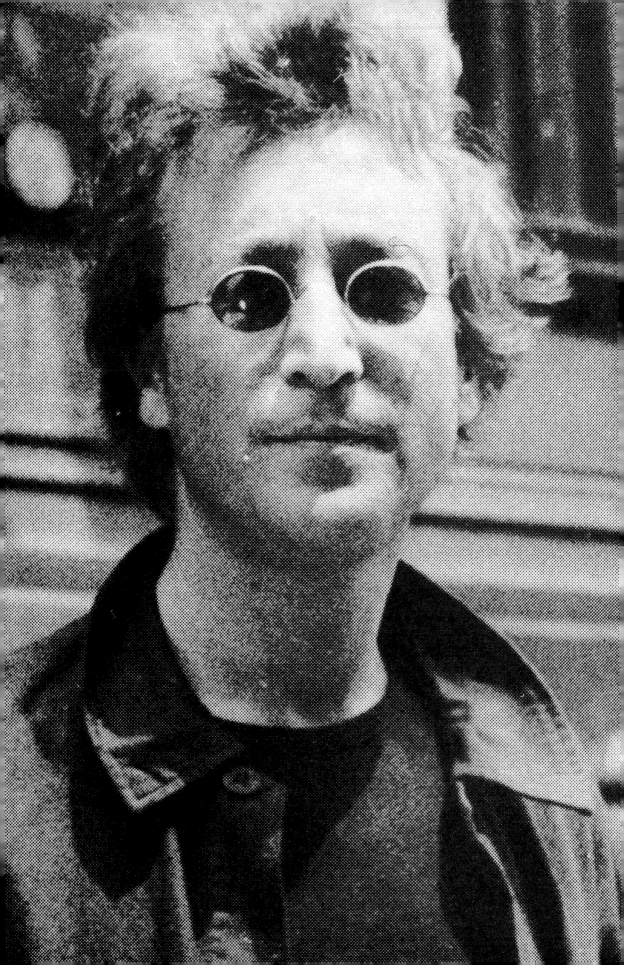

1976.

August 1976: Lennon appeared at the appeal session on his application for a green card to enable him to live in the USA. His original application was denied because of an old marijuana conviction in the UK: *Other than your original conviction, have you ever been convicted of any other crime?*
"No."
Were you ever a member of the Communist Party or any other organization that attempted to overthrow the United States government?
"No."
Do you intend to make the United States your home?
"I do."
What are your plans?
"I hope to continue living here with my family and make music."

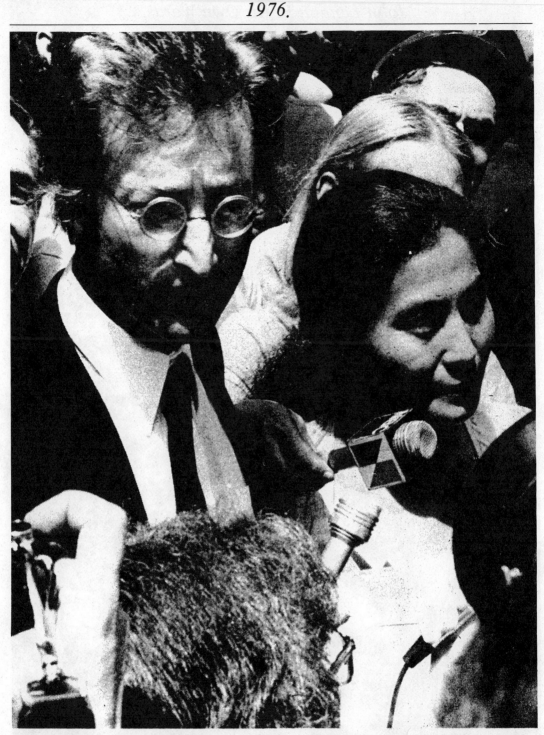

He was awarded a green card and made a statement to the court: "I'd like to publicly thank Yoko, my wife, for looking after me and pulling me together for four years, and giving birth to our son at the same time.

"There were many times that I wanted to quit, but she stopped me. I'd also like to thank a a cast of thousands, famous and unknown, who have been helping me publicly and privately for the last four years.

"And last but not least, I'd like to thank you, my attorney, Leon Wildes, for doing a good job well, and I hope this is the end of it."

Afterwards he said: I have a love for this country. Two thousand years ago, we would all have wanted to live in Rome. Not in the hills, but in Rome — and now, this is Rome. This is where the action is. I think we'll just go home, open a tea bag, and look at each other.

1979.

THE DAKOTA

Yoko took on the role of business manager while John brought up Sean: Well, sometimes, you know, she'd come home and say, "I'm tired." I'd say, only partly tongue in cheek, "What the fuck do you think *I* am? *I'm* 24 hours with the baby! Do you think that's easy?" I'd say, "You're going to take some more interest in the child." I don't care whether it's a father or a mother. When I'm going on about pimples and bones and which TV shows to let him watch, I would say, "Listen, this is important. I don't want to hear about your $20,000,000 deal tonight!" (*To Yoko*) I would like both parents to take care of the children, but how is a different matter.

The saying "You've come a long way, baby" applies more to me than to her. As Harry Nilsson says, "Everything is the opposite of what it is, isn't it?" It's men who've come a long way from even contemplating the idea of equality. But although there is this thing called the women's movement, society just took a laxative and they've just farted. They haven't really had a good shit yet. The seed was planted sometime in the late Sixties, right? But the real changes are coming. I am the one who has come a long way. I was the pig. And it is a relief not to be a pig. The pressures of being a pig were enormous.

I don't have any hankering to be looked upon as a sex obejct, a male, *macho* rock 'n' roll singer. I got over that a long time ago. I'm not even interested in projecting that. So I like it to be known that, yes, I looked after the baby and I made bread and I was a househusband and I am proud of it. It's the wave of the future and I'm glad to be in on the forefront of that, too.

Without Yoko I couldn't cope with life. I really need her and could not survive without her. She is the answer to everything. Being with her makes me whole. I don't want to be without her.

Our relationship is in part a teacher-pupil one. Few people understand that. She's the teacher and I'm the pupil. I'm the famous one, the one who's supposed to know everything, but she's my teacher. She taught me everything I know. From the day I met her she demanded equal time, equal space and equal rights. I'm thankful to her for my education.

People couldn't understand our relationship. They said she was a Japanese witch who had made me crazy. We're both sensitive people and we were hurt by all the criticism of Yoko. I couldn't understand why people wanted to throw rocks at her or punish me for being in love with her. As far as I was concerned I was with the person who was my goddess of love and the fulfilment of my whole life. Because of all the hosility there were a few times when we really went under but our love helped us survive.

It was harder for me to stop making music than for me to continue, although I don't think continuing would have done me any good artistically. I always liked hanging around the house; writing music meant hanging around the house. The only difference in the past five years was that instead of writing songs, I was writing menus.

I've been baking bread and looking after the baby. Everyone else who has asked me that question over the last few years says. "But what *else* have you been doing?" To which I say, "Are you kidding?" Because bread and babies, as every housewife knows, is a full-time job. After I made the loaves, I felt like I had conquered something. But as I watched the bread being eaten, I thought, Well, Jesus, don't I get a gold record or knighted or nothing?

I wanted to look after me and my family, that was the central concern. To be a family and not lose that was more important than creation and records and rock 'n' roll and being in Billboard. I cancelled all the trade papers, I didn't know what the hell was going on and I had no interest in it.

I never felt cut off. The point is, most people tend to feel that if you're not in the media, then you're not living. People said I was 'underground.' What the hell does that mean? I wasn't underground, I was living and overlooking the park.

This five years did as much good for me as it did for Sean. Look, I'd been *very* famous, and under great pressure, for 12 or 15 years, and I no longer wanted to churn out stuff that I thought was just *craftsmanship*. And when I decided to make music again, in the same way that I wanted to be with Sean, I wanted to make music with Yoko. She wanted to do it with me. We could have done it separately, she could have concentrated on making records, or being avant garde, or whatever, and I could have concentrated on being John Lennon. But what a bore. We automatically just wanted to do it together.

The New York Times, Sunday, May 27, 1979: A Love Letter From John And Yoko To People Who Ask Us What, When, And Why: The past 10 years we noticed everything we wished came true in its own time, good or bad, one way or the other. We kept telling each other that one of these days we would have to get organized and wish for only good things. Then our baby arrived! We were overjoyed and at the same time felt very responsible. Now our wishes would also affect *him*. We felt it was time for us to stop discussing and do something about our wishing process: The Spring Cleaning of our minds! It was a lot of work. We kept finding things in those old closets in our minds that we hadn't realized were still there, things we wished we hadn't found. As we did our cleaning, we also started to notice many wrongs things in our house: there was a shelf which should never have been there in the first place, a painting we grew to dislike, and there were the two dingy rooms, which became light and breezy when we broke the walls between them. We started to love the plants, which one of us originally thought were robbing the air from us! We began to enjoy the drum beat of the city which used to annoy us. We made a lot of mistakes and still do. In the past we spent a lot of energy in trying to get something. We still have a long way to go. It seems the more we get into cleaning, the faster the wishing and receiving process gets. The house is getting very comfortable now. Sean is beautiful. The plants are growing. The cats are purring. The town is shining, sun, rain or snow. We live in a beautiful universe. We are thankful every day for the plentifulness of our life. This is not a euphemism. We understand that we, the city, the country, the earth are facing very hard times, and there is panic in the air. Still the sun is shining and we are here together, and there is love between us, our city, the country, the earth. If two people like us can do what we are doing with our

lives, any miracle is possible! It's true we can do with a few big miracles right now. The thing is to recognize them when they come to you and to be thankful. First they come in a small way, in every day life, then they come in rivers, and in oceans. It's goin' to be alright! The future of the earth is up to all of us.

we thought we wanted, wondered why we didn't get it, only to find out that one or both of us didn't really want it. One day, we received a sudden rain of chocolates from people around the world. "Hey, what's this! We're not eating sugar stuff, are we?" "Who's wishing it?" We both laughed. We discovered that when two of us wished in unison, it happened faster. As the Good Book says — Where two are gathered together — It's true. Two is plenty. A Newclear Seed.

More and more we are starting to wish and pray. The things we have tried to achieve in the past by flashing a V sign, we try now through wishing. We are not doing this because it is simpler. Wishing is more effective than waving flags. It works. It's like magic. Magic is simple. Magic is real. The secret of it is to know that it is simple, and not kill it with an elaborate ritual which is a sign of insecurity. When somebody is angry with us, we draw a halo around his or her head in our minds. Does the person stop being angry then? Well, we don't know! We know, though, that when we draw a halo around a person, suddenly the person starts to look like an angel to us. This helps us to feel warm towards the person, reminds us that everyone has goodness inside, and that all people who come to us are angels in disguise, carrying messages and gifts to us from the Universe. Magic is logical. Try it sometime.

Many people are sending us vibes every day in letters, telegrams, taps on the gate, or just flowers and nice thoughts. We thank them all and appreciate them for respecting our quiet space, which we need. Thank you for all the love you send us. We feel it every day. We love you, too. We know you are concerned about us. That is nice. That's why you want to know what we are doing. That's why everybody is asking us What, When and Why. We understand. Well, this is what we've been doing., We hope that you have the same quiet space in your mind to make your own wishes come true.

If you think of us next time, remember, our silence is a silence of love and not of indifference. Remember, we are writing in the sky instead of on paper — that's our song. Lift your eyes and look up in the sky. There's our message. Lift your eyes again and look around you, and you will see that you are walking in the sky, which extends to the ground. We are all part of the sky, more so than of the ground. Remember, we love you.

John Lennon & Yoko Ono
May 27th, 1979
New York City

P.S. We noticed that three angels were looking over our shoulders when we wrote this!

1980.

1980: After a five year silence, John began to record again: The thing the '60s did was show us the possibility and the responsibility that we all had. It wasn't the answer. It just gave us a glimpse of the possibility.

And in the '70s everybody's going nah, nah, nah. And possibly, in the '80s, everyone will say, well, okay, let's project the positive side of life again.

You have to give thanks to God or whatever it is up there for the fact that we all survived. We all survived Vietnam or Watergate or the tremendous upheaval of the whole world. It's changed. We (the Beatles) were the hits of the '60s, but the world is not like the '60s.

I am going into an unknown future, but we're still all here. We're still wild about life, there's hope!

I'm talking to guys and gals who had been through what we had been through together, the '60s group that has survived...survived the war, the drugs, the politics, the violence on the street, the whole shabang. That we survived it, and we're here, and I'm talking to them, and the women's song is to Yoko, and it's to all women.

I'm more feminist now than I was when I sang 'Woman is the Nigger.' I was intellectually feminist then, but now I feel as though at least I've put, not my own money, but my body where my mouth is, and am living up to my own preachings, as it were.

You know, the words, 'All we are saying is give peace a chance,' literally came out of my mouth as a spoken word to a reporter, after being asked millions and millions of times, "What are you doing?"

Well, all I am saying is give peace a chance, not that I have the answer, or I have a new format for society because I don't, and I don't believe anybody else has.

It's like the channels on the radio were jammed. I wasn't geting clear signals. After 10, 15, almost 20 years of being under contract, and having to produce two albums a year and a single every three months, in the early days, regardless of what the hell else was doing, or what your family life was like or what your personal life was like, nothing counted you just had to get those songs up!

I don't want to have to sell my soul again, as it were, to have a hit record. I've discovered that I can live without it, and it makes it happier for me, but I'm not going to go back in and try to create a person who would not be myself.

I don't feel like 40. I feel like a kid. And I've got so many good years left ahead with Yoko and our son. At least, we're hoping so.

I hope the young kids like it as well but I'm really talking to the people who grew up with me. I'm saying "Here I am now. How are? How's your relationship going? Did you get through it all? Wasn't the seventies a drag, you know? Well, here we are, let's make the eighties great because it's up to us to make what we can of it''.

October 24, 1980: 'Starting Over' released: Why were people angry at me for not working? You know, if I was dead, they wouldn't be angry at me. If I'd conveniently died in the mid-'70s, after my *Rock and Roll* album or *Walls and Bridges*, they'd all be writing this worshipful stuff about what a great guy I was and all. But I didn't die, and it just infuriated people that I would live and just do what I wanted to do.

I'm going to have fun with it now, like I did when we first started. I never could have written *Starting Over* in 1975. I'm finding myself writing like I first used to write; these past five years helped me liberate myself from my own intellect, and my own image of myself. So, I could write again without consciously thinking about it, which was a joy.

This is like our first album. It's to say hi, hello, here we are. The next one will verify it, and then we'll start work on the third. It's fun to be rocking and rolling now, but if it gets not to be fun, then I'll just walk away. Because I know I can walk away now.

It's called 'Starting Over' because that's exactly what I am doing. It took me forty years to finally grow up. I see things now that I never knew existed before.

November 21, 1980: 'Double Fantasy' released: If I couldn't have worked with her, I wouldn't have bothered. I wouldn't enjoy just putting an album out by myself, having to do this by myself, have to go to the studio by myself.

After all, we're presenting ourselves as a couple,

and to work with your best friend is a joy, and I don't intend to stop it.

I started out doing rock and roll because I absolutely liked doing it. So that's why I ended up doing a track like 'Starting Over'. It's kinda tongue in cheek, it's kinda hoo-de-hoo-de-ho-ho ...sort of a la Elvis. I went back to my roots. I've had the boyhood thing of being the 'Elvis' and doing my own thing and getting my spot on the show. Now I want to be with my best friend — my best friend is my wife. Who could ask for anything more?

We feel like this is just a start now. You see, 'Double Fantasy' — this is our first album. I know we've worked together before, we've even made albums together before — but this is our first album. We feel, I feel, like nothing has ever happened before today!

John no longer used bodyguards when he went out: When I left England I still couldn't go on the street. It was still Carnaby Street and all that stuff was going on. We couldn't walk around the block and go to a restaurant unless you wanted to go with the business of 'the star going to the restaurant' garbage. Now, here, I've been walking the streets for the last seven years.

When we first moved to New York we actually lived in the Village, Greenwich Village, the arty farty section of town where all the students and the would-be's live, and a few old poets. Yoko told me, "Yes, you can walk on the street!" but I would be walking all tense-like, waiting for someone to say something or jump on me. It took me two years to unwind.

I can go out of this door now and go to a restaurant. Do you want to know how great that is? Or go to the movies? People come up ask for autographs or say "Hi!" but they won't bug you. They say "Howya doing? Like your record" or "Howya doing? How's the baby?"...

December 8, 1980: John Lennon gunned down outside his home in New York: What worries me is that one day a loony will come up and God knows what will happen then. Once when we were in Texas during an American tour, several shots were fired at our plane while it was parked on the tarmac. Maybe it was just jealous boyfriends or something but you never know in America. They're always running around with guns like a lot of cowboys. They think guns are extensions of their arms. (1965)

You know, I used to worry about death when I was a kid, now the fear of it means less and less to me. You know, when we were the rage we all used to use around-the-clock bodyguards because we genuinely feared for our lives. Now that we've been disbanded for so long, it's a great relief that the terror has disappeared from our lives. I would say that the only one of us that would have anything to worry about is Paul, because he's the only one left of the four of us who keeps increasing his profile. It seems as you get older, you worry less and less about death.

I think that I've had two lives. The first one ended wonderfully — and now the second is about to begin. I think — as marvelous as the first one was — the new one will be even better, because I am at more peace with myself and with Yoko. God, I almost lost her once, but that's going just fine now.

It took me a while to get things sorted out in my head, mate, but I now have a new — and *bigger* —direction to go in. It's a big, wide, wonderful world out there and Yoko and I are going to explore it until we die. I just have one hope: that I die before she does because we have become so much of an equation together that I don't think I would have the strength to go on without her.

Oh, I don't mean I would commit suicide; I just mean life would be so empty.

I hope I die before Yoko because if Yoko died I wouldn't know how to survive. I couldn't carry on.

We're going to live, or we're going to die. If we're dead, we're going to have to deal with that. If we're alive, we're going to have to deal with being alive. So worrying about whether Wall Street or the Apocalypse is going to come in the form of the great beast is not going to do us any good day today.

You have to do it yourself. That's what the great masters and mistresses have been saying ever since time began. They can point the way, leave signposts and little instructions in various books that are now called holy and worshipped for the cover of the book and not for what it says, but the instructions are all there for all to see, have always been and always will be. There's nothing new under the sun. All the roads lead to Rome. And people cannot provide it for you. I can't wake you up. *You* can wake you up. I can't cure you. *You* can cure you.

It's fear of the unknown. The unknown is what it is. And to be frightened of it is what sendseverybody scurrying around chasing dreams, illusions, wars, peace, love, hate, all that — it's all illusion. Unknown is what it is. Accept that it's unknown and it's plain sailing. Everything is unknown — then you're ahead of the game. That's what it is. Right?